# Female Anatomy and Sufferings



Author

**Ashok Kumar Rai**

DIAMOND BOOKS

www.diamondbook.in

**Publisher** : **Diamond Pocket Books (P) Ltd.**
X-30, Okhla Industrial Area, Phase-II
New Delhi-110020
Phone : 011- 40712200
E-mail : sales@dpb.in
Website : www.diamondbook.in
Printed by : Repro (India)

---

Female Anatomy and Sufferings

**Author : Ashok Kumar Rai**

*May Lord Shiva Bless on 50th Wedding Anniversary on 12th June, 2020*

# Dedication

- Dedicated to the sacred memory of my respected mother late Tapeshawari Devi Rai and father late Raj Rup Rai and also to all my ancestors with whose blessings I am what today.
- Dedicated to my Guru, I lay fragrant flower at the lotus feet of my graceful Gurus who blessed me with the light of knowledge.
- Dedicated to my younger brothers Mr. Prem Kumar Rai and Mr. Raj Kumar Rai and only beloved sister Ms. Induja Rai who have been caring and utmost supporting my life.
- Dedicated to my beloved son Mr. Sanjay Kumar Rai, daughter Ms. Kanchan Rai who have been caring and supporting me.
- Dedicated to my wife, Ms. Savitri Devi Rai who has given love to my life. Everything being done by her is a source of joy for me. I can never be sad when I'm around her.

# Acknowledgement

During my long professional journey of years1969-2009, I had the good fortune of working and interacting with professionals of high calibre from various institutions who constantly guided me in my career growth.

Some of the them are my "role model" and constant source of inspiration and motivation towards my success. Some of the eminent gentlemen who had come in my life are Shri P.S. Bami, Ex. CMD, NTPC, Shri H.L. Bajaj, Ex. CMD, CEA, Shri M.K. Sobti, Ex. Vice President Reliance Petrochemical, Late S.B. Kapoor, Ex. Director Engg. NTPC, Shri R.P.M. Tripathi, Ex. D.G. (Taxation). I express my sincere regard and deep gratitude to them.

A special thanks to Shri S.K. Aggarwal, Ex. Additional General Manager, NTPC for his kind cooperation, valuable advice and overwhelming support in my life whenever needed. I have all appreciation to his kindness of heart and kind gesture.

Last but not the least, I thank to my brothers, wife and children who has supported emotionally in my life and extended their valuable help when needed and given love to my life. I am obliged and indebted to my parents who had loved me a lot and guided me during the path of journey of my life.

# Foreword

A sincere effort had been made in this book to educate the reader about the female anatomy and sufferings. A frank sensitive and informative exploration of our life is a great mysterious and joys, related to the question about the sexuality, sexual health, relationship and aristocracy over female. Maintaining sexual health is an important part of our wellbeing. This book contains all information about the female anatomy, female sexual parts and emotional problems that can lead to dysfunction. This book covers all the sufferings - the marital discard, dowry, rape, domestic violence, murder, accident and acid attack. There are many problems in life being encountered with love and sex rooted in misinformation, lack of understanding or lack of communication.

Some people say that loving relationships between the sexes will always be problematic because of inherent difference between men and women. They say that men and women might be from different planets, men are from Mars and women are from Venus.

Without knowing their differences, the couple do not understand each other thus, no respect develops between them. We became demanding, resentful, judgemental and intolerant, happiness in love can only come when men and women make a conscious attempt to recognise and counter-act gender differences, women are the elite class of God's creation, therefore it is our mandatory responsibility to give respect and love them. Love is the main factor which binds the relationship of married life.

Love flows equals to blood flows and keep the heart free from attack.

**—Author**

# Contents

# Chapter-I
# Female Human Anatomy

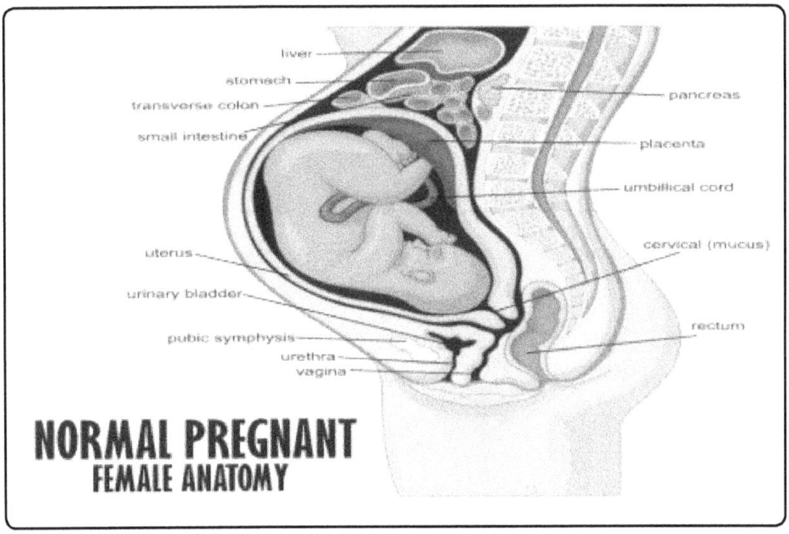

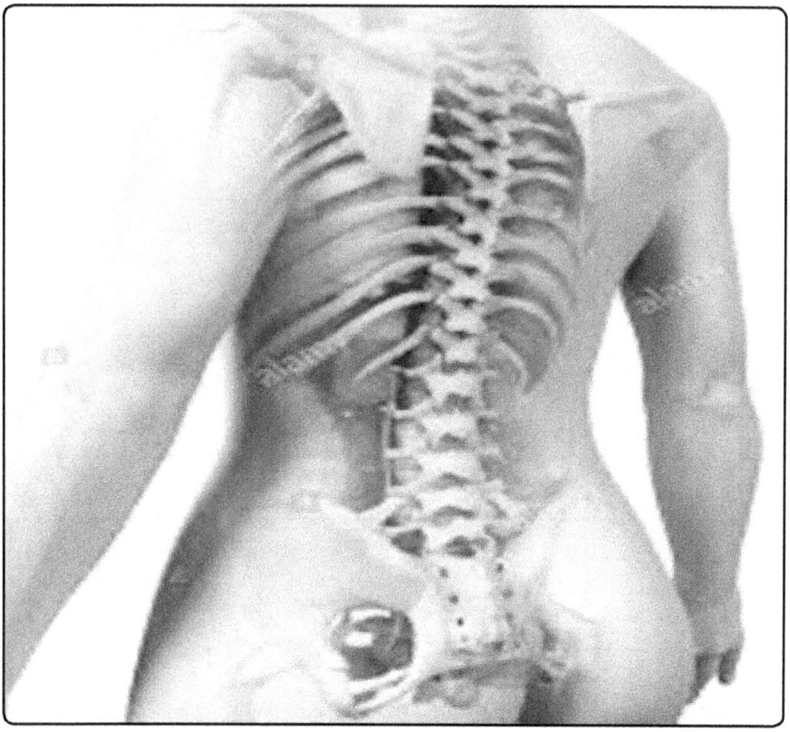

# Female Human Anatomy

## 1.0 Female Human Anatomy

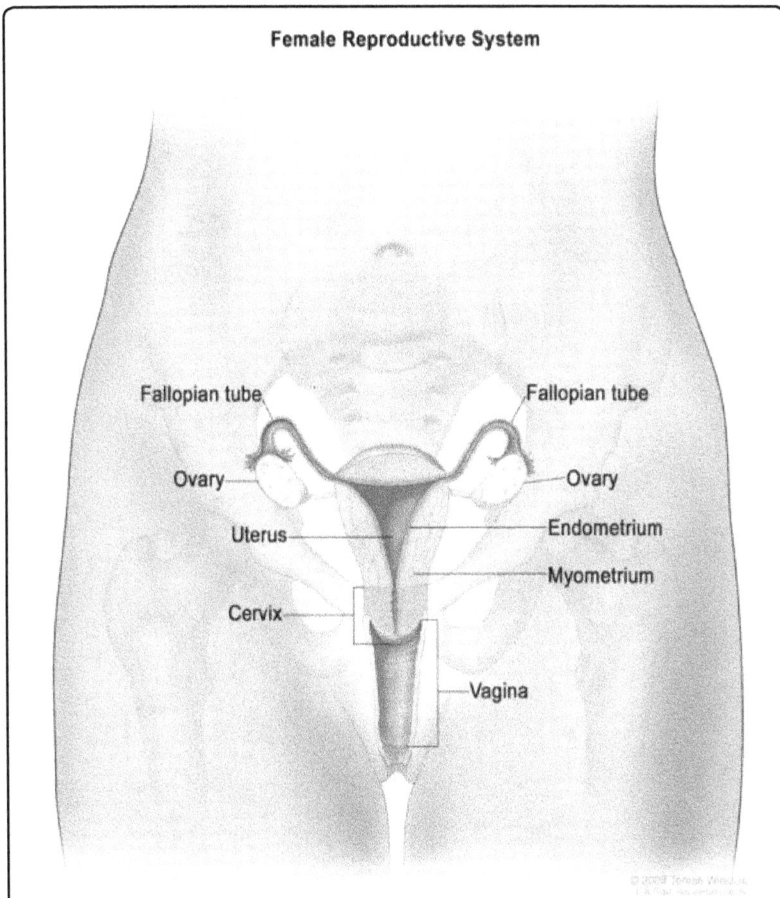

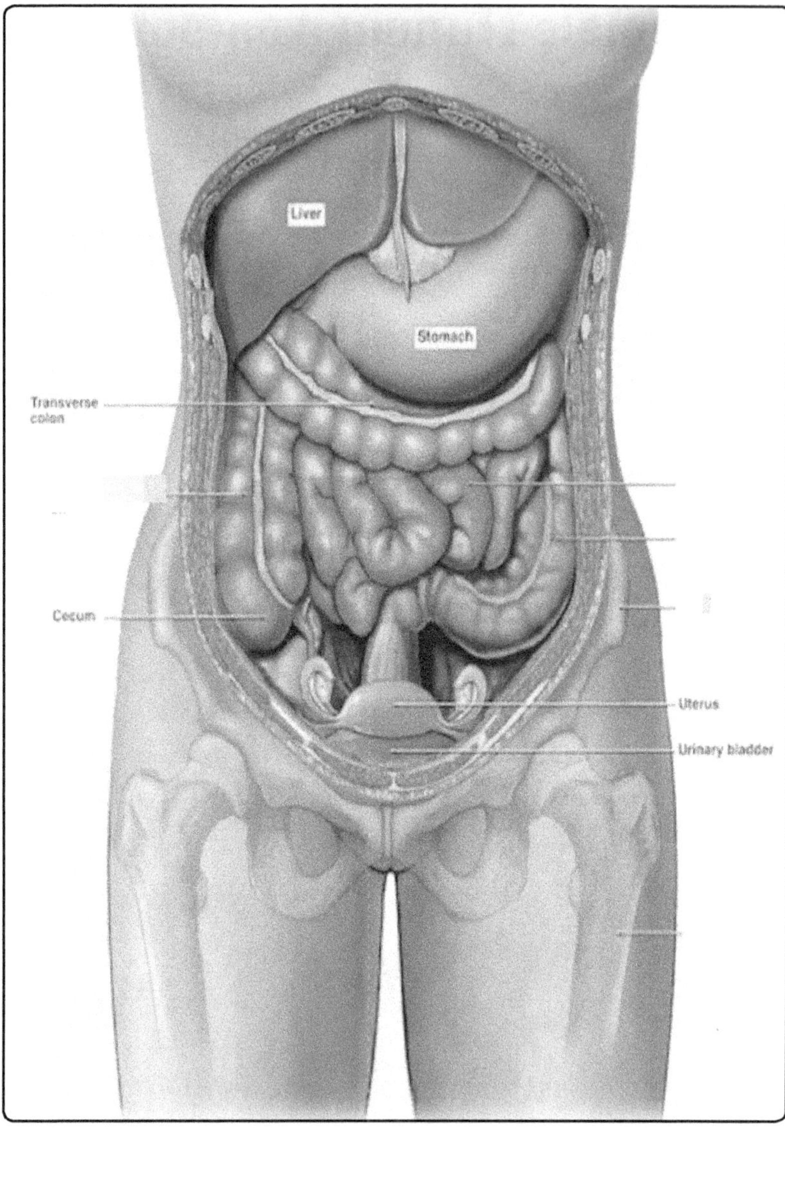
Liver
Stomach
Transverse colon
Cecum
Uterus
Urinary bladder

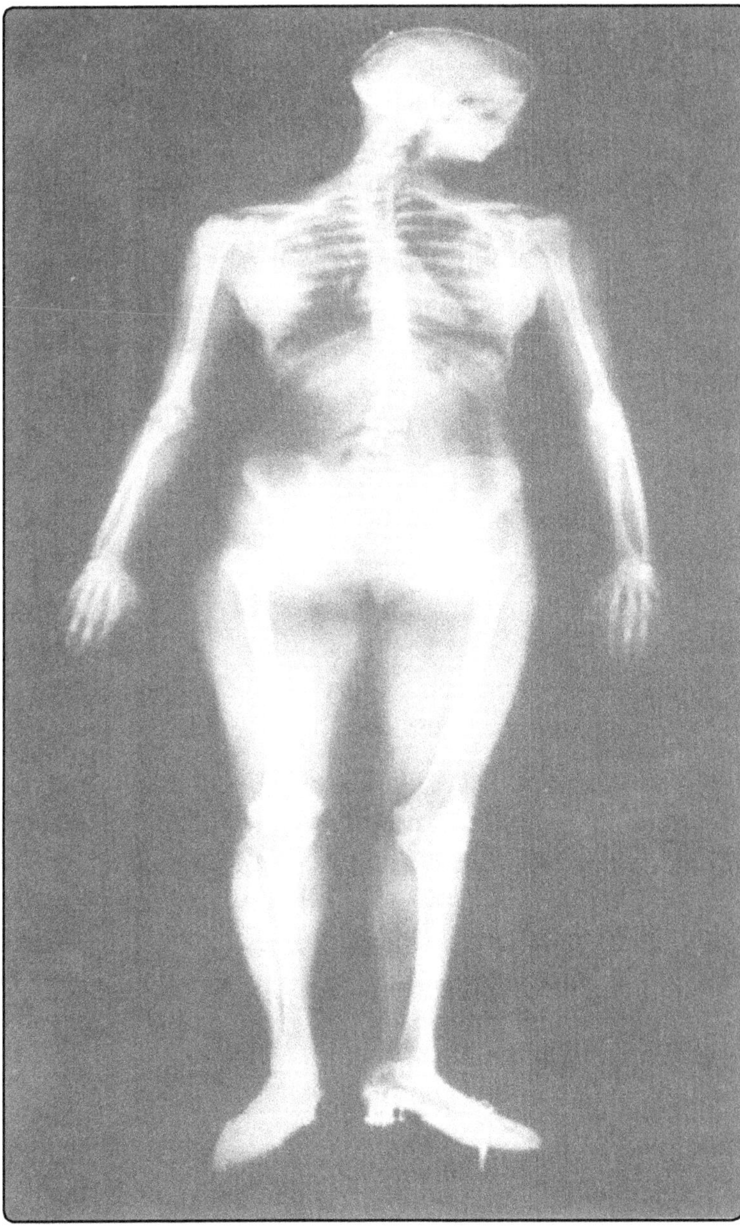

Bone structure of Female shown in X ray is different to Male structure

**Female Anatomy** includes the external genitals, or the vulva, and the internal reproductive organs, which include the ovaries and the uterus. One major difference between males and females is their reproductive organs. Anatomy specific to females generally relates to sexual function, reproduction, and hormone control. Males and females have physically different sexual anatomy, but all sex organs come from the same bundle of cells during foetal development. A baby's biological sex is determined at the moment the father's sperm meets the mother's egg. The vulva refers to the external parts of a female's genitals. It consists of several parts, including the labia majora, the labia minora, and the glans clitoris. The list below provides more detail on these parts.

- **Labia majora:** These are the fleshy outer lips on either side of the vaginal opening. The word "labia" is Latin for "lips." These outer lips usually grow pubic hair.
- **Labia minora:** These are the inner lips. They sit inside the outer lips but can be varying sizes. In some females, for example, the inner lips extend beyond the outer lips.
- **Clitoris:** The glans clitoris is at the top of the vulva, located where the inner lips meet. It is usually around the size of a pea, though size varies in females. Only the tip of the clitoris is visible, but it has two shafts that extend into the body by as much as 5 inches. The clitoris contains many nerve endings that are very sensitive, especially during sexual stimulation.
- **Clitoral hood:** The clitoral hood is the fold of skin that surrounds the head of the clitoris. It protects the clitoris from friction.
- **Urethral opening:** The opening to the urethra sits above the vaginal opening. The urethra connects to the bladder, and the opening is where urine exits the body.

- The uterus is located in the middle of the pelvic cavity. This muscular sac will house the foetus during pregnancy.
- During a female's monthly menstrual cycle, the lining of the uterus thickens with blood in preparation for the release of an egg from one of the ovaries. This is to prepare a nourishing environment for a foetus if pregnancy occurs.
- If pregnancy does not occur, the uterine lining sheds. This is called the menstrual period. It occurs after every around 28 days, though cycle length varies in females.
- The upper portion of the uterus is connected to the ovaries by the fallopian tubes.
- The ovaries are egg-shaped organs attached to fallopian tubes on the left and right sides of the body. Each ovary is roughly the size of an almond. Most females are born with two ovaries that produce eggs.
- In addition to producing eggs, the ovaries also produce hormones. Namely, they release oestrogen and progesterone.

## Fallopian Tubes

- The fallopian tubes connect the ovaries to the uterus. When the ovaries release an egg, the egg travels down the fallopian tube towards the uterus for potential fertilization.
- If a fertilized egg implants in the fallopian tube, doctors call this an ectopic pregnancy. An ectopic pregnancy is a medical emergency because the fallopian tube can rupture.

## Hymen

- The hymen is a membrane of tissue that covers the external vaginal opening.

- Not all females have a hymen. The hymen can rupture as a result of pelvic injury, sports activity, pelvic examination, cycling etc. The absence of a hymen does not mean that a female has lost her virginity.

## Female Ejaculation

- Female ejaculation is when a female's urethra expels fluid during sex. It can happen when a female becomes sexually aroused, but there is not necessarily an association with having an orgasm.
- Scientists do not fully understand female ejaculation, and there is limited research on how it works and its purpose. Female ejaculation is perfectly normal, although researchers remain divided on how many people experience it.

Female ejaculation refers to the expulsion of fluid from a female's urethra during orgasm or sexual arousal. The urethra is the duct that carries urine from the bladder to the outside of the body.

There are two different types of female ejaculation:

- **Squirting fluid:** This fluid is usually colourless and odourless and it occurs in large quantities.
- **Ejaculate fluid:** This type more closely resembles male semen. It is typically thick and appears milky.

Analysis has shown that the fluid contains prostatic acid phosphatase (PSA). PSA is an enzyme present in male semen that helps sperm motility.

In addition, female ejaculate usually contains fructose, which is a form of sugar. Fructose is also generally present in male semen where it acts as an energy source for sperm.

Experts believe that the PSA and fructose present in the fluid come from the Skene's glands. Other names for these glands include the paraurethral glands, Garter's duct, and female prostate.

Skene's glands sit on the front, inside wall of the vagina near the G-spot. Researchers believe that stimulation causes these glands to produce PSA and fructose, which then move into the urethra.

For many years, scientists thought that females who ejaculated during sex were experiencing continence problems. Research has since disproved this idea and confirmed the existence of female ejaculation. Is it normal and how common is it?

Female ejaculation is perfectly normal, yet people do not discuss it very often. According to the International Society for Sexual Medicine, different estimates suggest that between 10 and 50 percent of women ejaculate during sex.

Some experts believe that all women experience ejaculation, but many of them do not notice. It is possible that they are not aware of it because the fluid can flow backward into the bladder rather than leaving the body.

In a study that involved 233 women, 14 percent of participants reported that they ejaculated with all or most orgasms, while 54 percent said that they had experienced it at least once.

When the researchers compared urine samples from before and after orgasm, they found more PSA in the latter. They concluded that all females create ejaculate but do not always expel it. Instead, the ejaculate sometimes returns to the bladder, which then passes it during urination.

What is known is that the experience of female ejaculation, including the feeling, triggers, and amount of ejaculate, varies considerably from person to person. here is no evidence that female ejaculation has any health benefits. However, research has found sex itself to offer several benefits.

During orgasm, the body releases pain-relieving hormones that can help with back and leg pain, headaches, and menstrual cramps.

Immediately after climaxing, the body releases hormones that promote restful sleep. These hormones include prolactin and oxytocin.

Other health benefits include:

## Connection to the menstrual cycle

It is not clear whether or not there is a link between female ejaculation and the menstrual cycle. Some women say that they are more likely to ejaculate after ovulating and before menstruating, while others do not see a connection. More research is necessary to confirm or refute this association.

## Connection to Pregnancy

Some Scientists believe that female ejaculate plays a role in pregnancy. They think this because the fluid contains PSA and fructose, which help sperm on their journey toward an unfertilized egg. Others dispute this theory. They argue that ejaculate usually contains urine, which can kill sperm. They also say that it is not easy for the fluid to travel from the urethra to the vagina, where it would need to be to play a role in pregnancy.

### 1. The Vagina is not that part what you think

When you talk about the vagina, you might think you are referring to a woman's collective private parts, the word vagina actually refers to a specific part of the female reproductive system. It is the muscular tube that runs from the vulva — which refers to the external female genitalia, including the labia and clitoris — to the cervix. If you were wondering about size, research has found that vaginal depth can range from 2.7 to 3.1 inches. During sexual arousal, it is estimated that its depth can range from 4.3 to 4.7 inches.

### 2. Tampon lost

You may have heard some horror stories, but you'll be relieved to know that it is impossible to get a tampon lost in vagina; the opening at the top of vagina is simply too small for it to escape through. It is possible, however, to get a tampon stuck. If this is the case, you should see your doctor to get it removed. Leaving it in there for too long can increase the risk of toxic shock syndrome.

### 3. Vagina may get benefit from a workout

We are talking about pelvic floor exercises, which are otherwise known as Kegel exercises(named after Amold H. Kegel, American gynaecologist). They are normally done to help manage urinary incontinence, but research has shown that they can also help to improve sexual satisfaction. Kegel exercises help to tighten the vagina, making sex more pleasurable and more likely to lead to orgasm.

### 4. pH level of Vagina

The normal pH of the vagina is less than 4.5, which is similar to the pH of wine. *Lactobacilli* are the "good" bacteria that dominate the vagina; they help to keep pH levels normal in lady parts and prevent the growth of infection-causing bacteria. When levels of *lactobacilli* fall, vaginal pH levels can rise above 4.5, which is ideal breeding ground for vaginal infections, such as yeast infections and bacterial vaginosis.

### 5. Cleaning of Vagina

One should avoid using scented soaps and other perfumed products to clean vagina. Using such products interferes with the natural balance of vaginal bacteria, which may give rise to the aforementioned infections. In actual fact, we don't really need to be over-concerned with vaginal cleanliness at all; it takes care of itself. There are glands in the vagina that secrete fluid, or "discharge," and this helps to keep it clean. "I see women of all ages with irritation, soreness, and itching," said Dr. Sangeeta Agnihotri (Gyn. & Obs.), "Because there is a tendency for women to be overzealous with their cleanliness. This causes discomfort." The vagina is sensitive area. It is recommended to wash once a day with water," she added.

**6. Clitoris has thousands of Nerves**

While the clitoris is not a part of the vagina, but it is considered by many women as the crux of sexual pleasure, and it's no wonder; the tip of the clitoris alone has a whopping 8,000 nerve endings — more than double the number of nerve endings in the penis — making it the most sensitive part of a woman's erogenous zone. Researcher has revealed that the clitoris can increase in size by up to 300 percent during sexual arousal.

**7. Vagina does not Fart**

All women have experienced it at one point or another that embarrassing yet uncontrollable emission of air from the vagina, which is commonly known as "queefing". Yes, queefing sounds a lot like farting, but sounds can be deceiving. Those little puffs of air that emerge from lady parts are simply that — trapped air that is being released from the vaginal canal. They are not "farts" in the traditional sense because they are not waste gases, nor do they emit an unpleasant odor. That said, in some rare cases, vaginal flatulence may be caused by a vaginal fistula, which is an abnormal opening from the vagina to the bladder, colon, or rectum.

**8. The link between Vagina and Shark**

Vagina can be compared with Shark fish, lady parts have more in common with Sharks. The lubricant produced by the vagina contains a compound called squalene, which is the same compound that is found in the livers of Sharks. Controversially, squalene is also used in many cosmetic products, such as moisturizing lotions, sunscreens, and hair products.

**9. About the G-spot**

The G-spot — an erogenous zone of the vagina that, when stimulated, may lead to sexual arousal and orgasm.

The G-spot is believed to be located deep inside the vagina, between the cervix and the bladder. The G-spot is a relatively new discovery by Malaysian researcher Dr. Chua Chee Ann. In a study, he reported that 10–15 minutes of G-spot stimulation led to instant orgasms and vaginal lubrication in 15 percent of women who reported pain and dryness during sexual intercourse.

# 1.1 Female Genitals

Women's genitals, including the clitoris, labia, vagina, G-spot and cervix provide sexual pleasure for women and their partners. The vagina itself is literally the passageway from which new life emerges. Learning about these body parts—what they're called, where they are, and what they do—is important for women's sexual health and pleasure.

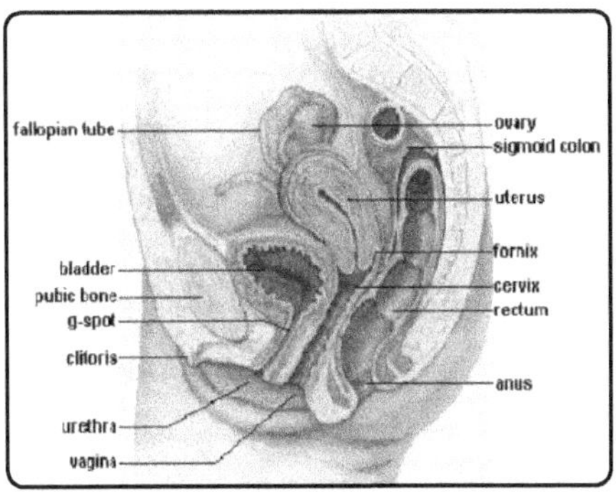


The external area of the female genitals (the parts you can see in the picture) is sometimes mistakenly called the vagina. However, the correct term for these outside parts is the vulva. It includes the mons pubis (which is the mound of tissue that forms a triangle between a woman's legs and is covered with pubic hair), the labia majora (outer vaginal lips), labia minora (inner vaginal lips) and the clitoris and clitoral hood. It is important to note that not all vulvas look the same; women's labia, in particular, come in numerous different shapes, sizes and colours. Also, just like our eyes and ears, the labia are usually not symmetrical.

# 1.2 Uterus

The uterus is shaped like an upside-down pear, with a thick lining and muscular walls. Located near the floor of the pelvic cavity, it is hollow to allow a blastocyte, or fertilized egg, to implant and grow. It also allows for the inner lining of the uterus to build up until a fertilized egg is implanted, or it is sloughed off during menses.

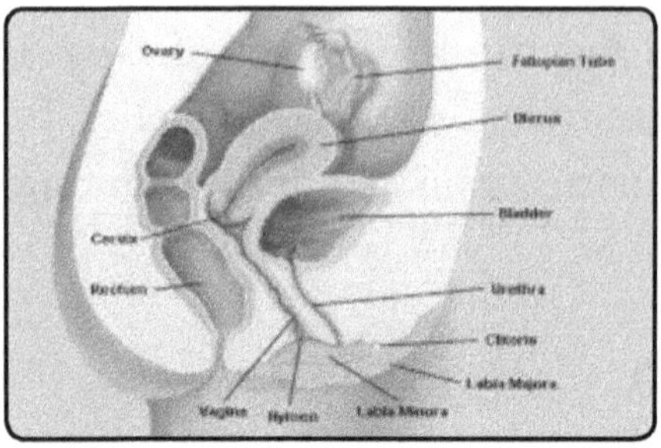


The uterus contains some of the strongest muscles in the female body. These muscles are able to expand and contract to accommodate a growing foetus and then help push the baby out during labor. These muscles also contract rhythmically during an orgasm in a wave like action. It is thought that this is to help push or guide the sperm up the uterus to the fallopian tubes where fertilization may be possible.

The uterus is only about three inches long and two inches wide, but during pregnancy it changes rapidly and dramatically. The top rim of the uterus is called the fundus and is a landmark for many doctors to track the progress of a pregnancy. The uterine cavity refers to the fundus of the uterus. Helping support the uterus are ligaments that attach from the body of the uterus to the pelvic wall and abdominal wall. During pregnancy the ligaments prolapse due to the growing uterus, but retract after childbirth. In some cases, after menopause, they may lose elasticity and uterine prolapse may occur. This can be fixed with surgery.

Some problems of the uterus include uterine fibroids, pelvic pain (including endometriosis, adenomyosis), pelvic relaxation (or prolapse), heavy or abnormal menstrual bleeding, and cancer. It is only after all alternative options have been considered that surgery is recommended in these cases. This surgery is called hysterectomy. Hysterectomy is the removal of the uterus, and may include the removal of one or both of the ovaries.

## 1.3 Fallopian Tube

At the upper corners of the uterus are the fallopian tubes.

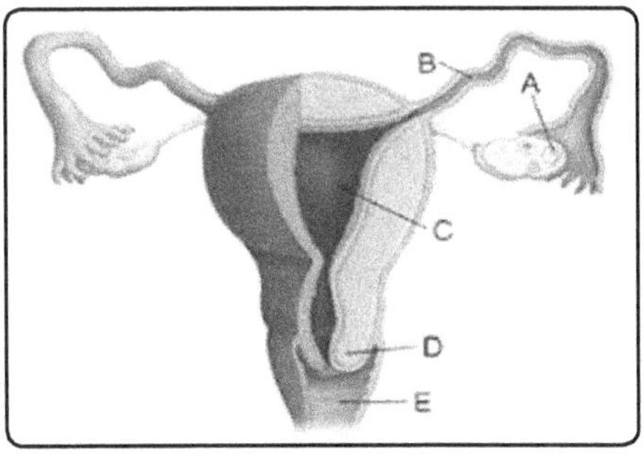


There are two fallopian tubes, also called the uterine tubes or the oviducts. Each fallopian tube attaches to a side of the uterus and connects to an ovary. They are positioned between the ligaments that support the uterus. The fallopian tubes are about four inches long and about as wide as a piece of spaghetti. Within each tube is a tiny passageway no wider than a sewing needle. At the other end of each fallopian tube is a fringed area that looks like a funnel. This fringed area, called the infundibulum, lies close to the ovary, but is not attached. The ovaries alternately release an egg. When an ovary does ovulate, or release an egg, it is swept into the lumen of the fallopian tube by the fimbriae.

Once the egg is in the fallopian tube, tiny hairs in the tube's lining help push it down the narrow passageway toward the uterus. The oocyte, or developing egg cell, takes four to five days to travel down the length of the fallopian tube. If enough sperms are ejaculated during sexual intercourse and there is an oocyte in the fallopian tube, fertilization will occur. After fertilization occurs, the zygote or fertilized egg, will continue down to the uterus and implant itself in the uterine wall where it will grow and develop.

If a zygote doesn't move down to the uterus and implants itself in the fallopian tube, it is called a ectopic or tubal pregnancy. If this occurs, the pregnancy will need to be terminated to prevent permanent damage to the fallopian tube, possible haemorrhage and possible death of the mother.

# 1.4 Mammary Glands

Many people consider breasts "accessory organs" to the female reproductive system, as they are responsible for supplying milk to an infant after childbirth.

The major external components of the breasts include the:

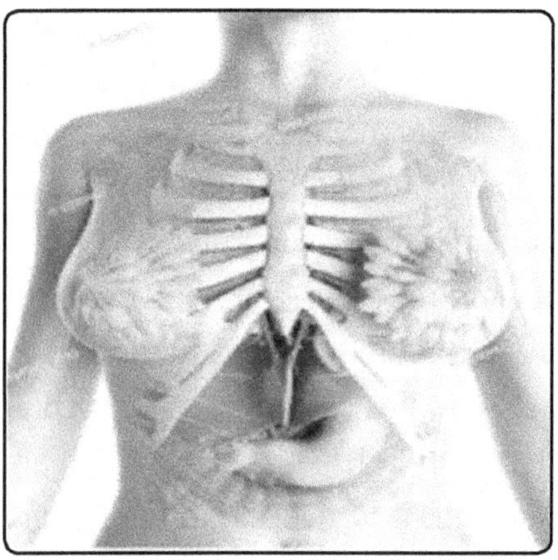

**Nipple:** The nipple is the rounded area where milk drains to feed a baby. They have many nerve endings that can make them an area of sexual stimulation. Nipples do not always protrude. Some females have flat or inverted nipples.

**Areola:** The areola is the pigmented area that surrounds the nipple. It is circular and varies in size from person to person. It contains small glands, called Montgomery glands, that secrete lubrication to keep the nipple from drying out, especially when nursing.

**Breast tissue:** The breast is the area of skin on the chest that is composed of fat, muscle, and ligament tissue, as well as an intricate network of blood vessels and glands. These areas are specialized for breastfeeding. Breast tissue size varies greatly from person to person, often due to a combination of individual genetics and body mass.

Internally, the breasts are primarily composed of fat. The amount of fat can determine breast size. However, breast size has no bearing on the amount of milk someone is able to produce.

The internal anatomy of the breasts includes the:

**Alveoli:** These are milk secreting cells grouped into clusters inside the breasts.

**Lactiferous ducts:** These are special channels that open on the nipple's surface. Breast milk exits through these ducts to nourish a baby.

**Lobules:** These are collections of alveoli in the breast that secrete milk. The lobules drain into lactiferous ducts, then into lactiferous sinuses that promote milk flow from the nipple.

Mammary glands are the organs that produce milk for the sustenance of a baby. These exocrine glands are enlarged and modified sweat glands.

## Structure

The basic components of the mammary gland are the alveoli (hollow cavities, a few millimetres large) lined with milk-secreting epithelial cells and surrounded by myoepithelial cells. These alveoli join up to form groups known as lobules, and each lobule has a lactiferous duct that drains into openings in the nipple. The myoepithelial cells can contract, similar to muscle cells, and thereby push the milk from the alveoli through the lactiferous ducts towards the nipple, where it collects in widenings (sinuses) of the ducts. A suckling baby essentially squeezes the milk out of these sinuses.

The development of mammary glands is controlled by hormones. The mammary glands exist in both sexes, but they are rudimentary until puberty when - in response to ovarian hormones - they begin to develop in the female. Oestrogen promotes formation, while testosterone inhibits it.

At the time of birth, the baby has lactiferous ducts but no alveoli. Little branching occurs before puberty when ovarian oestrogens stimulate branching differentiation of the ducts into spherical masses of cells that will become alveoli. True secretory alveoli only develop in pregnancy, where rising levels of oestrogen and progesterone cause further branching and differentiation of the duct cells, together with an increase in adipose tissue and a richer blood flow.

Colostrum is secreted in late pregnancy and for the first few days after giving birth. True milk secretion (lactation) begins a few days later due to a reduction in circulating progesterone and the presence of the hormone prolactin. The suckling of the baby causes the release of the hormone oxytocin which stimulates contraction of the myoepithelial cells.

The cells of mammary glands can easily be induced to grow and multiply by hormones. If this growth runs out of control, cancer results. Almost all instances of breast cancer originate in the lobules or ducts of the mammary gland.

## 1.5 Female Sexual Dysfunction

The definition of the word Libido is one's psychic energy that is put towards making the person's development. The Libido is affected by both physical and emotional or psychological factors.

The amount of libido varies from person to person and even in the same person, libido is different from one age to another. Mentally, libido is controlled by societal expectations and notions of what male and female relationships should be. Decrease in libido is a disturbance affecting treated hypertensive subjects of both sexes.

While it's true that sex is a physical act, libido is built on emotions in women. Libido is also high when women are going through their initial pubertal changes, such as development of breasts and nipples.

**Sexual Disorders:** Human sexual functioning consists of the complex interaction of the vascular, nervous and endocrine system which interact to produce sexual desire and arousal. There are four stage model, the four stages are excitement, plateau, orgasm, and resolution. Excitement is characterized by the one set sexual feelings. During this stage, blood pressure and heart rate increases, male experience erection and in female vaginal lubrication occurs. The second stage, plateau is characterized by more advance stage of arousal. The third stage, orgasm is a reflex brought about by vasocongestion and myotonia. For men, semen is ejaculated from the penis and for women, reflex rhythmic contractions of the circumvaginal muscles occur, the final stage is termed as the resolution stage, in which specific physical response return back to resting position.

**Refractory period sex:** In human sexuality, the refractory period is usually the recovery phase after orgasm during which it is physiologically impossible for a man to have additional orgasms. This phase begins immediately after ejaculation and lasts until the excitement phase of the human sexual response cycle begins a new with low level response.

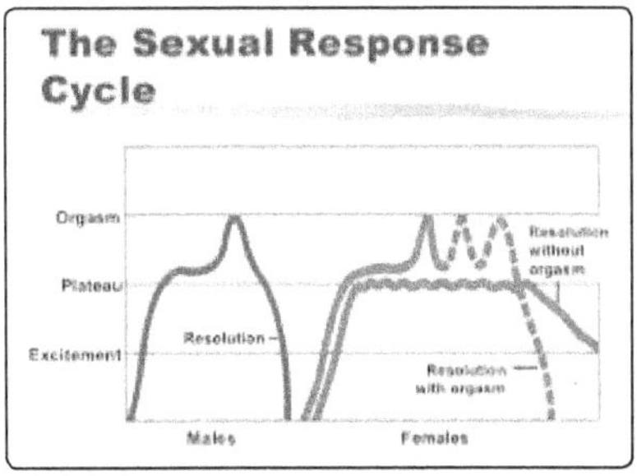

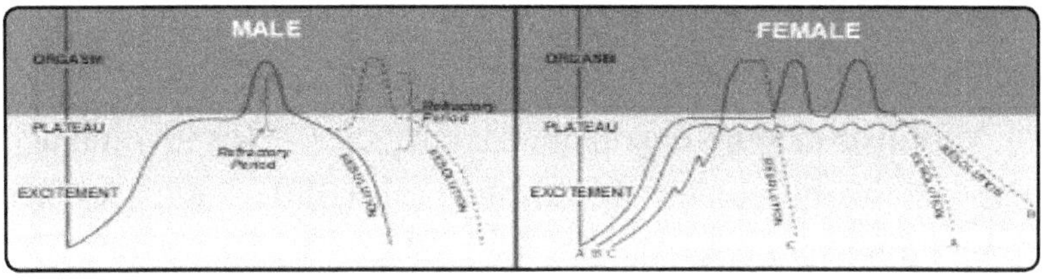

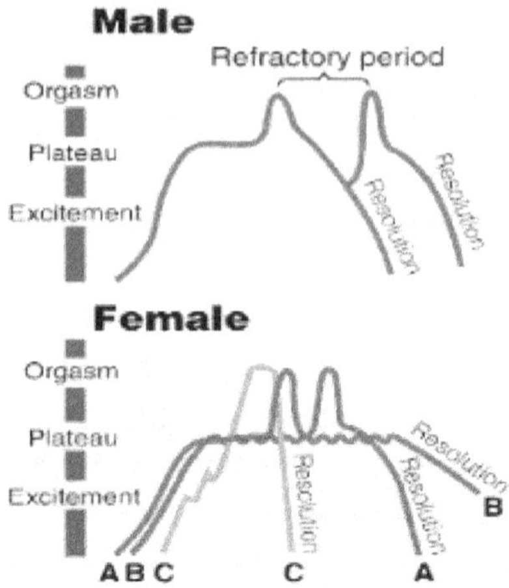


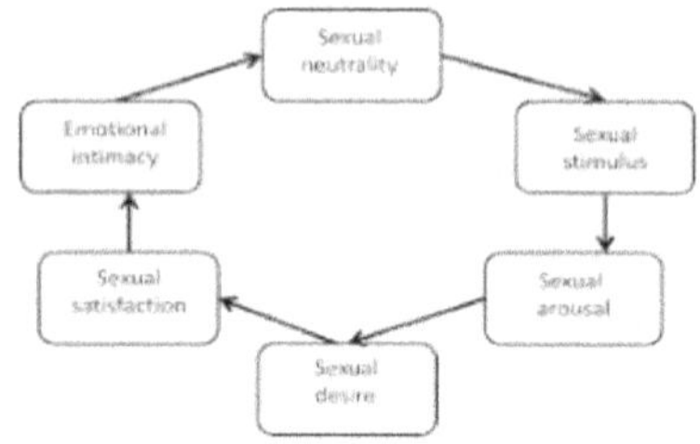


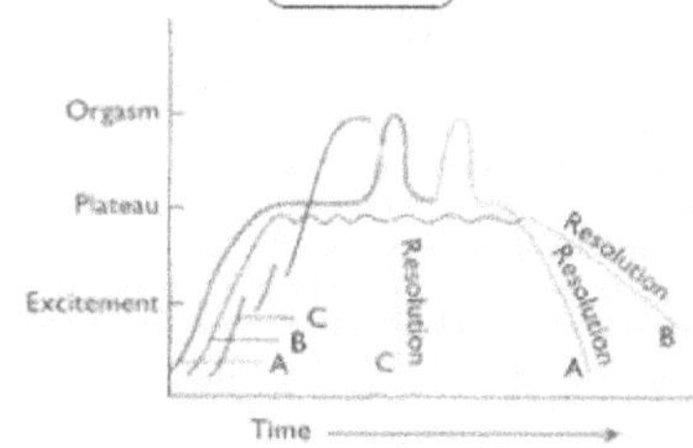


**Hypoactive sexual desire:** This disorder is inhibited sexual desire, usually the patient of this disorder reports absence of sexual fantasies and lack of desire or interest to engage in sexual activities.

**Sexual aversion disorder:** This disorder is characterized by a persistent aversion to and avoidance of genital sexual contact with a sexual partner.

**Female sexual arousal disorder:** Characterised by recurrent partial or complete failure to attain or maintain the lubrication-swelling response of the sexual excitement stage of human sexual response and also the patient reports that lack of sense of sexual pleasure during sexual activity.

**Inhibited Female orgasm:** This dysfunction is characterized by a persistent or recurrent pattern in which a woman does not experience an orgasm subsequent to adequate sexual stimulation and excitement experience, a delayed orgasm following such excitement stimulation.

**Vaginismus:** This dysfunction is characterised by involuntary spasm of the musculature of the outer third of the vagina so that penetration is not possible.

### Libido Enhancement

Women have been conditioned to be so quiet about sexual issues that the word 'female libido enhancement' has only recently cropped up. Female libido enhancement and women's sexuality in general was a little bit ignored compared to male impotence problems until now. Women have just as much right to female libido enhancement as men have to male sexual enhancement.

Female libido enhancement is far from a new concept. The Chinese developed libido enhancement for both genders centuries ago as an answer to creating a more well-rounded sexual life for all citizens. The Romans, the Greeks, and civilizations before and since have always found special uses for female libido enhancement. Scientific evidence has proven that the age-old remedies used for centuries have stood the test of time, and the notion of female libido enhancement can now be contained in a bottle.

### Conclusion

Female Libido is complex and may result from both medical and psychological conditions. In the past, it was a subject that was unknown however female libido enhancement is becoming even more well known. If you and your partner do suspect that libido is not all it could or should be, a low testosterone level is the likely culprit. Another fact of female libido is that more sex actually can increase your desire for sex.

## 1.6 Why Women think less about Sex?

The female brain is actually wired to be different from its male counterpart. The female brain sees the world differently and reacts differently to old age from the male brain in every stage of life from new-born. Research shows that most aspects of male and female brain are similar, IQs average is the same, both sexes are capable of excellence and physical, artistic and intelligent pursuits. There also are fascinating difference. The brain scan shows they use different brain circuitry to find the solution. Women tend to have faster and broader verbal skills, women have more neurons in the part of the brain devoted to emotion and to detecting emotion in others, In complex situation, women is likely to understand the overall situation better than men. There is a neurological reasons why women think less about sex than men. How she is wired, genetic wiring and brain chemistry make women different from men, the differences are fascinating, a close look at various parts of the female brain as follows:

1. **Prefrontal Cortex-Self Control:** Aggressive impulses originating in amygdala, part of the brain. It is larger and matures in women, so they tend to more patient than man.

2. **Insula-Intuition:** The key to gut instincts. It is bigger in women making them better at reading nonverbal cues such as facial expressions.

3. **Anterior Cingulate Cortex-Anxiety:** Larger in women, so they are prone to worry.

4. **Hippocampus-Emotional Memory:** Bigger and more active in women, no wonder, they remember emotional event in detail.

5. **Hypothalamus-Control Hormones:** It becomes active earlier in women. Hence they enter puberty sooner and more sensitive to hormone fluctuations.

6. **Pituitary Gland-Mother instincts:** Work in society hypothalamus to control hormone gland, triggers milk production during pregnancy.

7. **Amygdala-Aggression:** Anger and fear originate here. It is smaller in women. So they are less likely to take physical risks.

## 1.7 Perception Beauty of Female

Beauty is not in the eye of the beholder, it's in the values of the beholder. It turns out that female beauty is simply the representation of our values. The fact that woman's beauty is the representation of our values also made it possible to finally illuminate what the source of beauty's strange and unrelenting power over us has always been.

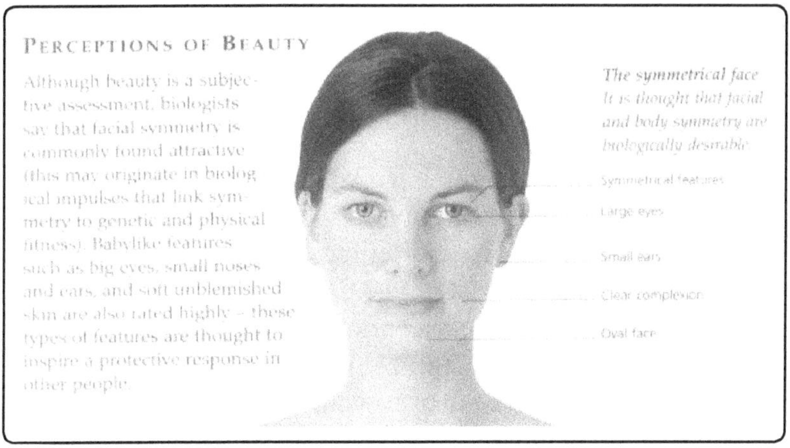


People are learning that female beauty is a God-like quality, and that the men who uphold its value are heroes. When her beauty is attacked, it is by twisted monsters bent on destroying all human values, the things female beauty represents to all of us.

## 1.8 Understand the Female Body Language

### 1. Withdrawing Attention

- If she pushes her fingers through her hair, she is looking to get your attention. The way she touches her hair is also very important. It tells you information about her temperament. If she does it slowly, you have encountered a cunning expert of the art of love. Quick, nervy movements disclose impatience or embarrassment.

- If she touches the edge of the glass with her fingers, Freudian psychologists often interpret it as a sexual sign. This theory is supported by the women themselves, who claim that they deliberately pet the glass, in order to call the chosen man's attention upon themselves. Elegant, caressing movement is a sign of intrinsic calmness, self-control and waiting, so sit by her. Her beating a rhythm on the glass with her nails is a sign of impatience or a broad hint of SOS, which she's sending to her boyfriend, who is fighting for another Bailey's at the bar.

## 2. Note any Physical Contact

- If she touches you in any manner, this is almost always a good sign with the exception of the event in which she is striking you and telling you to get out. If she is lightly touching you on the arm, this is almost always a good sign, with the exception of the event in which she is striking you and telling you to get out. If she is lightly touching you on the arm while laughing, or in general just finding any way she can touch you on your bump, or grab you, then she is almost certainly interested.

## 3. Check out her Hands and Arms

- If she leans on her hand with her chin and her eyes seem to be thinking, it's not always the sign of her being impressed by your appearance. Generally, the woman tries to answer her own question this way.You know the answer, but the lady needs time. If you want to help her make the only right decision, be politely determinate and determinately polite. Flash your sense of humour as well.
- If she sits back with her arms crossed together, she may be uncomfortable with her weight or she might be annoyed. This is the worst possible thing you can encounter when out hunting. This gesture is evidence

of the fact that you've made the worst impression of all on the woman and she doesn't trust you at all. Nothing helps here, neither refined jokes, nor nice, muscular body. The only thing that may help in this situation is to pull back away from her, lean back, and lean away. Turn away from her if you cannot lean back. Show her that you're not interested in her. Turn back and smile to her if she is opening up, do it progressively. Tell her that you'll have to go soon, and sit/stand there talking with her. Let her see that you're charming to other people, talk with other woman/people, let her miss you. If this is the case, maybe she'll come back.

- The way the woman herself thinks of her hands is also very important. If she stares at them for a very long time, it may imply that likes you and is nervous. If she is very shy, she will not be able to look at you. Another reason for this behaviour is that something angers. If she beats the rhythm on the table or the bar means a similar state of mind.

## 4. Look at the Lips

- If a woman wets her lips quite frequently, it's either out of habit or desire to get you to pay attention to her lips and sooner or later kiss her.
- When a woman is biting her lips, do not interrupt her – everything is alright. But sometimes, when she's biting them, you may assume that she's nervous. Why? Perhaps you are staring at her too inquisitively, or she is subtly.

## 5. Eye the Eyes

According to famous experts of the topic and authors of cheap romantic stories, the fast movement of the eye-lashes is the sign of women who like to conquer men of their own accord.

Besides, they are emancipated, who like to take over the duty of

initiation. They aren't waiting for your jokes and wide smile. They undertake to initiate. The only problem with such ladies is that not all of them will enjoy herself in the role of the doped-out game. But if you don't mind losing the role of the hunter, swallow the bait. Also, note her pupils. Basic biology tells us that when we like something (or someone) our pupils expand (dilate). When we don't like something, they contract. If her pupils are big, it may be a sign that she likes you, or likes what you're saying. On the other hand, if her pupils are small and pointed, it may be a bad sign. However, this method isn't fool proof. If it is really bright outside pupils' contract naturally, regardless and if you are somewhere darker, they naturally dilate.

## 6. Check out the Legs

Researchers of body language emphasize that when a woman frequently crosses her legs let them swing, is also a sexually charged movement. The strongest of all these movements is when she opens her legs without meaning it. It's a classical Freudian opening symbol. A contrary sign to this is when she puts her legs together.

## 7. Look at her Feet

If her feet are pointed at you, this means she is interested in you. But, if not, tell her something that will catch her attention.

# Chapter-II
# Parenting of Girl Child

# Parenting of Girl Child

## 2.0 Parenting of Girl Child

The parents want their children to be healthy. As elementary

school aged children go through remarkable physical changes of all kinds, their food intake becomes a critical aspect of this growth and development. Recent research shows that nourishing food not only makes a child healthier, it makes him emotionally more stable, and it improves school performance. It appears then that paying attention to our children's diets pays high dividends. If only our children thought so, too! Because children tend to rank their parents' views on food along with their unpopular views on curfews, rock music, hair styles, etc., it is up to the parents to, first of all, be clever about insinuating nutritious foods into the family menus and, secondly, take a reasonable but hard line when other approaches fail.

## 2.1 Parents as a Role Model

Many psychologists feel that the first relationship a baby forms, usually with the mother, sets the pattern for all future relationship in that child's life. While the ability to love does not require high intelligence. It is the exchange with each other. The children absorb the relationship pattern that exist among the rest of family. The way other members of family communicate and giving respect to child, it has a profound

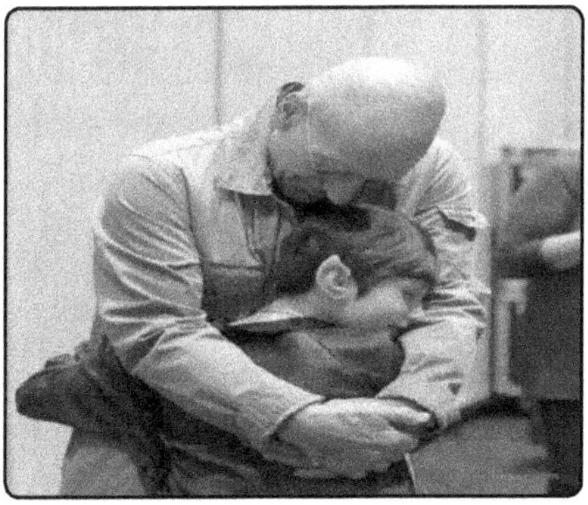

influence on a child. The opposite sex parent takes a more significant role as the boy starts to become conscious of his or her own sexuality. In contrast, the constant presence of a nurturing mother and father provides the best environment in which to raise a child. When divorce or death intervened, resulting in a single- parent family, the effect on the child's eventual long-term adult relationship can range from minimal to devastating.

## 2.2 Multiple Birth

A multiple birth is the culmination of one multiple pregnancy, wherein the mother delivers two or more offspring. A term most applicable to vertebrate species, multiple births occur in most kinds of mammals, with varying frequencies. Such births are often named according to the number of offspring, as in *twins* and *triplets*. A multiple pregnancy may be the result of the fertilization of a single egg that then splits to create identical fetuses, or it may be the result of the fertilization of multiple eggs that create fraternal fetuses, or it may be a combination of these factors. A multiple pregnancy from a single zygote is called *monozygotic*, from two zygotes is called *dizygotic*, or from three or more zygotes is called *polyzygotic*. Similarly, the siblings themselves from a multiple birth may be referred to as monozygotic if they are identical or as polyzygotic if they are fraternal.

Each fertilized egg (zygote) may produce a single embryo, or it may split into two or more embryos, each carrying the same genetic material. Foetuses resulting from different zygotes are called *fraternal* and share only 50% of their genetic material, as ordinary full siblings from separate births do. Foetuses resulting from the same zygote share 100% of their genetic material and hence are called identical. Identical twins are always the same sex, except in cases of Klinefelter syndrome (also known as XXY syndrome and 47, XXY syndrome).

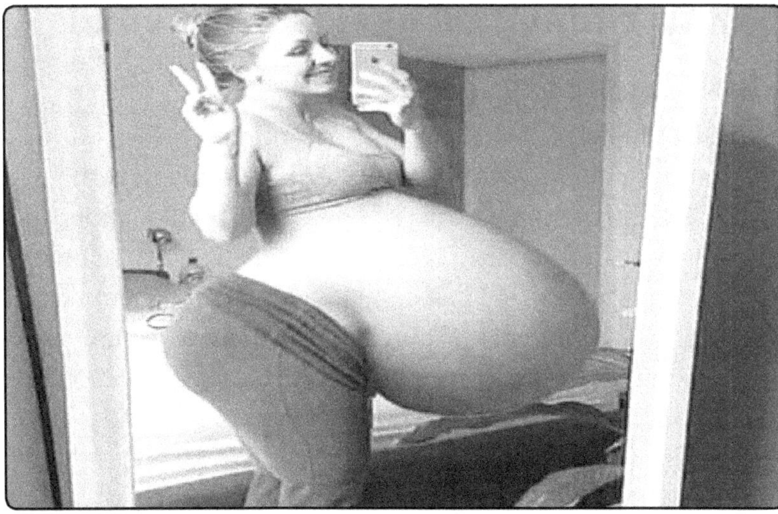

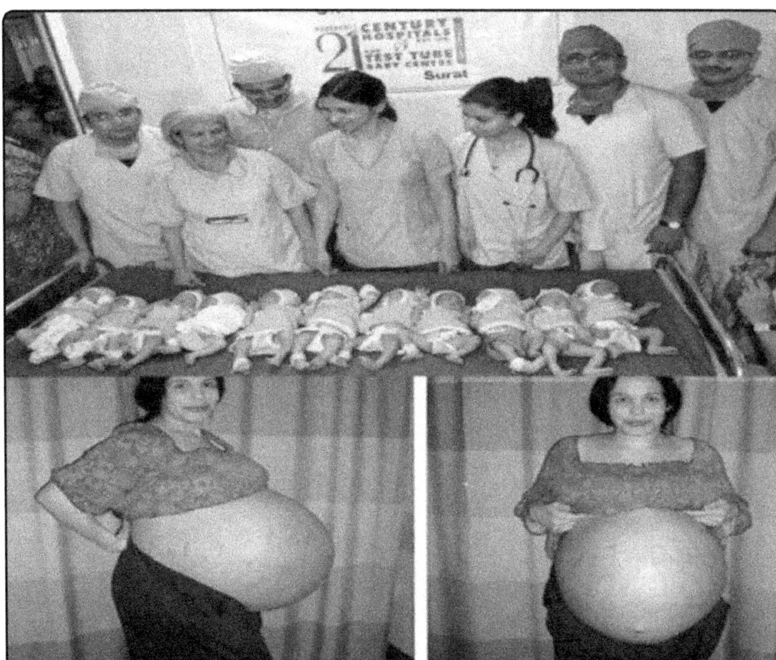
21
CENTURY
HOSPITALS
TEST TUBE
Surat

## 2.3 Discrimination against the Female Child

While children around the world continue to face various forms of adversity in the 21$^{st}$ century, girl children in particular are subjected to multiple forms of oppression, exploitation, and discrimination due to their gender. United Nations statistics, national reports and studies initiated by Non-Governmental Organizations repeatedly show that girls, as a group, have lower literacy rates, receive less health care, and are more often impoverished than boys. It is also important to note these conditions, more often than not, do not improve as girls grow to become women, discrimination against girl children are numerous and vary depending on the traditions, history, and culture of a particular society.

# Chapter-III
# Cruelty to Female Child

# Cruelty to Female Child

## 3.0 Female Infanticide

### Female Foetuses dumped in well in Patiala

Infanticide is the homicide of an infant. Generally, it is female infanticide as it is more prevalent than male infanticide. Recently, 15 aborted foetuses. It was recovered from well in Patiala from well located behind a Nursing home sent a shock wave across Punjab which was already fighting a losing battle with an adverse ratio.

The foetuses were recovered from Sahib nursing home in Patran town following the raid of Police and Health Authority Sources said that at least 35 foetuses of female were thrown in the well in three months.

In the global scenario India is becoming a force to reckon with and we are very proud of this fact. But there are some home truths that we are unaware of female infanticides and sex selective abortions.

## 3.1 Selective Abortion and Infanticide

India has a highly masculine sex ratio, the chief reason being that many women die before reaching adulthood. Tribal societies in India have a less masculine sex ratio than all other caste groups. This, in spite of the fact that tribal communities have far lower levels of income, literacy and health facilities. It is, therefore, suggested by many experts, that the highly masculine sex ratio in India can be attributed to female infanticides and sex-selective abortions.

All medical tests that can be used to determine the sex of the child have been banned in India, due to incidents of these tests being used to get rid of unwanted female children before birth. Female infanticide (killing of girl infants) is still prevalent in some rural areas. The abuse of the dowry tradition has been one of the main reasons for sex-selective abortions and female infanticides in India.

## 3.2 Killing of Female Child in Rajasthan

Female infanticide is a deliberate and intentional act of killing a female child within one year of its birth either directly by using poisonous organic and inorganic chemicals or indirectly by deliberate neglect to feed the infant by either one of the parents or other family members. On the other hand, female foeticide is the termination of the life of a foetus within the womb on the grounds that its sex is female and is also known as sex selective abortion.

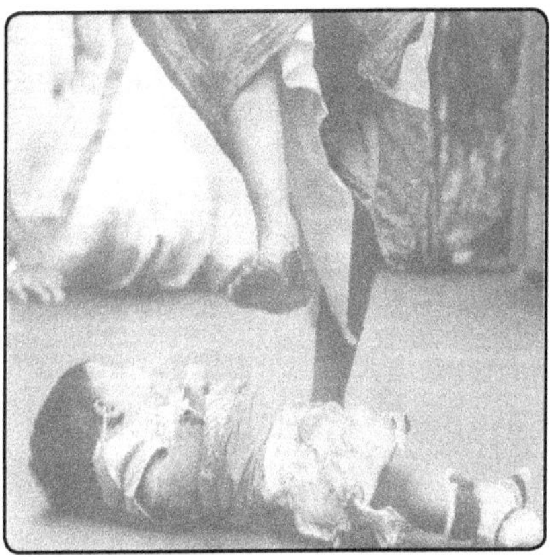

Female infanticide can also be defined as killing of an entirely dependent child under "one year of age who is killed by mother, parents or others in whose care the child is entrusted". It has been reported that female infanticide existed in India since 1789 in several districts of Rajasthan; along the Western shores in Gujarat – Surat and Kutch; and among a clan of Rajputs in Eastern part of Uttar Pradesh. It was so rampant in Kutch that only five of such families were found who had not killed their new-born daughters. Today there are alarming reports of the baby girls being murdered even in areas where this practice did not exist earlier. Poverty, ignorance of family planning, cost of dowry, etc. have been reported as the possible causes for this crime.

## 3.3 Poisoning of Female Child

Conjunction of two ethical evils: Abortion and gender bias.

In this the girl become target of attack even before they are born. The practice of female foeticide is based on the sex determination by testing the amniotic fluid while the woman is pregnant. Such tests are banned in India but they are secretly and unethically carried out by some medical professionals. If the foetus is a female it is more often than not aborted. In fact, in a well-known Abortion Centre in Mumbai, after undertaking the sex determination tests, out of the 15,914 abortions performed during 1984-85 almost 100 per cent were those of girl foetuses. Similarly, a survey report of women's centre in Mumbai found that out of 8,000 foetuses aborted in six city hospitals 7,999 foetuses were of girls. It has also been reported that about 4,000 female babies are aborted in Tamil Nadu every year. Also female foeticide has replaced female infanticide as a means to reduce or eliminate female offspring as in societies where women's status is very low, many female foetuses are rejected. Female foeticide and infanticide have adversely affected Indian society.

## 3.4 Two Days Girl Child Saved from Grave

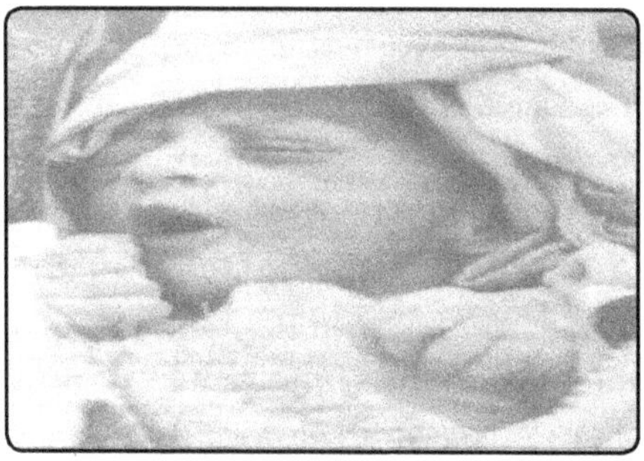

The biggest and most easily measurable effect is the low female-to-male ratios. It is so great that today 36 percent of men between the ages of 15yrs. and 45yrs. in the wealthy state of Haryana are unmarried. This prevalence of unmarried men has a destabilizing effect that counteracts the stabilizing and enriching effects of families in a society. In fact according to census statistics the number of female infants comparing to male infants has dropped from 972 girls per 1000 boys in 1901 and 929 girls per 1000 boys in 1991.

The number of girls is continuously decreasing and if no initiative is taken then there may be a time when we will have no girls in India. But cases like these only go ahead to show how big and deep rooted the problem is – many baby girls were brutally murdered in Rajasthan in March 2010, One-day-old girl thrown into canal was found alive in Kurukshetra in 2008 and obsessed with the desire to give birth to a son, a frustrated mother killed all her three daughters in Odisha in 2007.

## 3.5 Female Genital Cutting

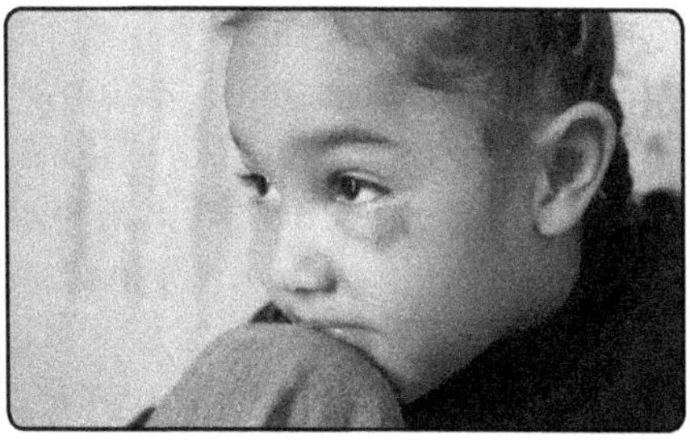

Female Genital Cutting (FGC) refers to any practice that involves the removal or the alteration of the female genitalia. It is a centuries-old cultural practice found in many countries among people following various religions and beliefs, but is most prevalent in Africa.

Other terms for FGC include female genital mutilation, female genital circumcision, female genital operations, or clitoridectomies.

According to the United Nations Population Fund, "it is estimated that over 130 million girls and women have undergone some form of genital cutting and at least two million girls are at risk of undergoing the practice every year." FGC is reportedly practiced in 28 of Africa's 43 countries, most pervasive in Egypt, Eritrea, Mali, Sudan, and the Central African Republic. In the Middle East, FGC is found in Oman, Yemen, and the United Arab Emirates. Some immigrant populations in the United States, Latin America, and Asia (Indonesia, Sri Lanka, and Malaysia) practice FGC as well.

Studies done in areas where FGC is widespread suggest there is a direct correlation between a women's attitude toward FGC and her place of residence, educational background, and work status. According to the results of a health survey in Egypt, urban women are less likely than rural women to support FGC. There was less support for FGC among women who were employed and among women who had at least a secondary-level education.

## 3.6 Female Genital Mutilation

Female Genital mutilation (FGM) is the practice of cutting away the parts of external female genital. It is usually called female circumcision by those who practice it. There are three broad categories of FGM are: clitoridectomy, excision and infibulation.

Excision includes the removal of clitoris and cutting of labia minora. The most extreme FGM is infibulation, the removal of clitoris and labia. The mildest form of FGM is clitoridectomy, removal of clitoris. The excision includes the removal of clitoris and cutting of labia minora, and the stitching together of the labia majora. Infibulation leaves just a small opening in the vagina for the passage of urine and menstrual fluid, and requires binding together of the legs until stitches adhere. Often the removal of the stitches is part of a wedding night ritual. The U.N. agency, the United Nations Children's Fund (UNICEF), reports that FGM is "normally performed by traditional practitioners with crude instruments, such as knives, razor blades and broken glass, usually without anaesthetics."

The invasive nature of FGM and the unsanitary conditions under which it is usually performed can have serious consequences. Public Health Magazine writes that "FGM may cause numerous physical complications, including haemorrhage and severe pain, which can cause shock, even death." It also writes that "FGM may create long-term complications resulting from scarring and interference with the drainage of urine and menstrual blood, such as chronic pelvic infections, which may cause pelvic and back pain, dysmenorrhea, infertility, chronic urinary tract infections, urinary stones, or kidney damage." The magazine also writes that "FGM may create long-term complications resulting from scarring and interference with the drainage of urine and menstrual blood, such as chronic pelvic infections, urinary stones, or kidney damage." Infibulation is especially dangerous during childbirth when women who have been infibulated are "at risk of prolonged labor, which may lead to fetal brain damage or fetal death.

## 3.7 Parental Sex Selection

The discriminatory practice of prenatal sex selection, or sex-selective abortion, occurs when the sex of a foetus is the determining factor in whether that foetus will be aborted or continued. Prenatal sex selection is a two-step process. Step one involves identifying the sex of the foetus through amniocentesis, chorionic villus sampling, or ultrasound. Step two consists of aborting the foetus based solely on the identification of the fetus as female. While prenatal sex selection may be done for medical reasons (for example, to prevent sex-specific genetic disorders such as haemophilia), it is also based on cultural and discriminatory considerations.

## 3.8 Child Abuse or Child Maltreatment

Maltreatment is physical, sexual or psychological maltreatment or neglect of a child or children, especially by a parent or a caretaker. Child abuse may include any act or failure to act by a parent or a caretaker that results in actual or potential harm to a child, and can occur in a child's home, or in the organizations, schools or communities the child interacts with.

The terms child abuse and child maltreatment are often used interchangeably, although some researchers make a distinction between them, treating child maltreatment as an umbrella term to cover neglect, exploitation, and trafficking. Different jurisdictions have developed their own stances towards mandatory reporting, different definitions of what constitutes child abuse for the purposes of removing children from their families or for prosecuting a criminal charge.

## 3.9 Sexual Abuse

### Child sexual abuse (CSA)

Child sexual abuse (CSA) is a form of child abuse in which an adult or older adolescent abuses a child for sexual stimulation. Sexual abuse refers to the participation of a child in a sexual act aimed toward the physical gratification or the financial profit of the person committing the act. Forms of CSA include asking or pressuring a child to engage in sexual activities (regardless of the outcome), indecent exposure of the genitals to a child, displaying pornography to a child, actual sexual contact with a child, physical contact with the child's genitals, viewing of the child's genitalia without physical contact, or using a child to produce child pornography. Selling the sexual services of children may be viewed and treated as child abuse rather than simple incarceration.

Effects of child sexual abuse on the victims include guilt and self-blame, flashbacks, nightmares, insomnia, fear of things associated with the abuse (including objects, smells, places, doctor's visits, etc.), self-esteem difficulties, sexual dysfunction, chronic pain, addiction, self-injury, suicidal ideation, somatic complaints, depression, post-traumatic stress disorder, anxiety, other mental illnesses including borderline personality disorder and dissociative identity disorder, propensity to re-victimization in adulthood, bulimia nervosa, and physical injury to the child, among other problems. Children who are the victims are also at an increased risk of sexually transmitted infections due to their immature immune systems and a high potential for mucosal tears during forced sexual contact. Sexual victimization at a young age has been correlated with several risk factors for contracting HIV including decreased knowledge of sexual topics, increased prevalence of HIV, engagement in risky sexual practices, condom avoidance, lower knowledge of safe sex practices, frequent changing of sexual partners, and more years of sexual activity.

## 3.10 Forced Child Marriage

Forced child marriages entrap women and young girls in relationships that deprive them of their basic human rights. Forced marriage constitutes a human rights violation in and of itself. The convention on consent to marriage recalls that the Universal Declaration of Human Rights states that "marriage shall be entered into only with the free and full consent of the intending spouses prescribed by law." The Convention goes on to state that "State Parties to the present Convention shall take legislative action to specify a minimum age for marriage. No marriage shall be legally entered into by any person under this age, except where a competent authority has granted a dispensation as to age, for serious reasons, in the interest of the intending spouses."

## Sexual Exploitation, Prostitution, and Trafficking

Sexual exploitation, trafficking, and prostitution present significant risks to the girl child's mental and physical health. Numerous countries and organizations, including the United States and the United Nations, have monitored and begun initiatives to end the practices.

## Crimes Committed in the Name of "Honor"

Thousands of girl children around the world are killed each year for committing or being capable of committing transgressions deemed to be dishonourable. "Honor" killings are defined by the Human Rights Watch as "acts of violence, usually murder, committed by male family members against female family members who are perceived to have brought dishonor upon the family."

Motives for "honor" killings have included: Suspicion of adultery, premarital sex, or some other relationship between a woman and a man, being a victim of rape or sexual assault, refusing to enter an arranged marriage, seeking divorce or trying to escape marital violence, and falling in love with someone who is unacceptable to the victim's family according to the Global Campaign to stop killing and stoning women.

Sexual Harassment is a violation of women's human rights and a prohibited form of violence against women. Sexual harassment causes incalculable economic, psychological and physical harm to its victims and serves to reinforce the subordination of women to men in the workplace. Sexual harassment against the girl child is prevalent both in the workplace and at school. Girl children who are employed as domestic workers or as industrial laborers are vulnerable to sexual harassment and exploitation by their employers. Girl children who attend school are often victimized by teachers or their peers.

## 3.11 Female Infanticide and Sex-Selective Abortion

Female infanticide is the murder of a young girl child, often occurring as a deliberate murder of a girl infant or young girl child or as the result of neglect. Selective abortion – also called gender-selective abortion, sex-selective abortion, or female foeticide – is the abortion of a foetus because it is female. Medical technology has made it possible for parents to discover the sex of a foetus at earlier and earlier stages of pregnancy, so many women from communities with a preference for boy practice selective abortion.

These practices occur most frequently in societies where a girl child is viewed as culturally and economically less beneficial than a boy child. Female infanticide has been reported in China, North Korea, South Asia (Bangladesh, India, Nepal, Pakistan), the Middle East (Algeria, Egypt, Jordan, Libya, Morocco, Syria, Tunisia, Turkey) and parts of Africa (Cameroon, Liberia, Madagascar, Senegal, Nigeria).

Female infanticide and foeticide are predominantly practised in regions of significant poverty and over population. One reason boys are more valued than girls is preserving lineage, as family lineage and family name are carried only by males in most societies. Also, children are expected to care for parents in their old age in many countries, so raising a son becomes a better investment because once a girl marries, she has to take care of her husband and his family, and of virtually no value to her parents. Some women resort to female infanticide and foeticide in order to protect their daughters from a life of objectification and subjugation in a male dominated society, where there is a prevalent anti-girl attitude.

Economically, girls often have a lower earning potential than boys, as boys are more likely to find work and receive higher pay. This is significant in poor communities where each family member is expected to add to the household income. A girl can no longer contribute to her family's income after marriage when she must turn all of her wages over to her husband. In many situations, it is much more of an economic burden to raise a girl, as many cultures require religious and social ceremonies for girls but not boys. Holding a proper ceremony for the purpose of maintaining respectable social stature can be very expensive, often leaving poor families with nothing.

Mothers are not the only perpetrators of female infanticide and foeticide, as more dominant members of the immediate family, such as the husband or mother-in-law, often encourage or carry out the deed. In addition, women may experience pressure from members of their community, possibly facing physical abuse, disownment from their husband or parents, and homelessness if they choose to keep a child against the direction of others.

An alarming information on female infanticide and selective abortion has come from the world's two most populous nations: India and China. Both countries are predominantly patriarchal, and it is the cultural norm for a girl to leave her family for her husband's after marriage. India continues the practice of dowry, although illegal, which makes female children especially undesirable as large sums of money must be paid at the time of marriage. For this reason, female infanticide is especially prevalent in rural areas and among lower castes. In China, with the induction of the People's Republic in 1949, the practice of female infanticide was largely abandoned. However, cases of missing women increased in the 1980s, a phenomenon correlated with the one child policy that was launched in 1979 to control exorbitant population growth. With this stringent law, many families chose to keep a boy child over a girl child because they believe sons can take care of their parents in old age, while daughters are handed over to another person's family.

Ex-selective abortion and female infanticide have had consequences beyond the loss of many females' lives. They have contributed to the dramatic change in the ratio of men to women in some countries. As fewer men can find women to marry in societies where these practices are widespread, the trafficking of women from foreign countries to sell as wives has become a profitable business. Some adoption agencies take advantage of the devaluation of girls and solicit impoverished families to sell their daughters so they may be adopted overseas.

Countries like India and China have criminalized female infanticide, although local law enforcement often ignores cases. For example, many doctors in China and India, whose practices are limited to providing sex-selective abortion, are not reprimanded. As legislation and law enforcement cannot guarantee the elimination of these practices, public awareness of the issues and grassroots support of local communities are essential to prevent and eradicate female infanticide and sex-selective abortion. Progress has been made in India where the government has taken steps to implement programs to educate the public and have encouraged NGOs to take action against these practices.

## 3.12 Child Abuse Study in India

The 'Study on Child abuse India 2007' conducted by the Ministry of Women and Child Development acknowledges that child sex abuse takes place in schools. One out of two children in schools have faced sexual abuse. And overall, more boys than girls face various forms of sexual abuse - ranging from inappropriate touch, exposure to pornography or violent sexual assault. "The abuser could be from the peer group or an older student," says Dr. Loveleen Kacker, Joint Secretary (Child Welfare) in the Women and Child Development Ministry, who prepared the government report. "Senior students often bring pornographic material to school and may force a younger boy to look at it to titillate themselves.

During a study on child abuse in Kolkata, Elaan, an NGO, found that four out of 10 boys faced sexual harassment in school. Generally, the age of maximum abuse cases is between 9 to 12 years. The national study found that the abuse gained momentum at the age of 10 years and peaked between 12 to 15 years. Child abuse is the physical or psychological maltreatment of a child by an adult often synonymous with the term child maltreatment or the term child abuse and neglect. There are many forms of abuse and neglect and many governments have developed their own legal definition of what constitutes child maltreatment for the purposes of removing a child or prosecuting a criminal charge. The report by the Department of Women and Child Development on the implementation of the Convention of Child Rights in India, prepared for the United Nations Committee on the Rights of the Children, has identified child sexual abuse as a priority issue for immediate action. A Belgianatholic Church-backed commission published a report on September 10, 2010 revealing hundreds of cases of alleged sexual abuse of minors by clergy and church workers, and 13 suicides by abused victims. The Commission said that it had received 475 complaints in the first six months of this year from alleged victims or their families. Most were related to charges of sexual abuse committed between the 1950s and the late 1980s by Catholic Clergy, but also by teachers of religion and adults working with youth movements.

## Child, Sex, Tourism

India has become one of the hottest child sex tourism destination. A report, trafficking in women and children in India, sponsored by the National Human Rights Commission (NHRC), highlights this, mentioning not just Goa, which since the 1990s, has uncovered rackets by Freddy Peats and Helmut Brinkmann, but also Alleppy and Ernakulam districts of Kerala, where houseboat tourism has lately seen a boom. But the reports finding tell only part of story. "The attention paedophiles are paying to India is preposterous," says Rakesh Gupta, a child rights activist. "They are mentioning the Golden Triangle- Delhi, Agra and Jaipur - in their anonymous blog posts."

In Kerala, "sex on the water" is the latest rage for paedophiles. Most paedophiles heading for Kerala started in Delhi, where police estimate the existence of 10 cartels specialising in child sex tourism. "With nearly a lakh homeless child in Capital, it's easy for paedophiles to come and expolit them" says Dr Rajat Mitra, who heads Swanchetan, an NGO specialising rape trauma. In Mumbai, nearly 70,000 minors are abused yearly, estimates Kusumbar Choudhury to save the children in India.

## Child Abuse Statistics

There are 5,00,000 children in prostitution, in India. More than 3 children die a day in the USA. Of the total number of children who were killed in the USA, from 1976-1997, 54 percent were killed by a parent, 15 percent were killed by strangers or unknown persons. There are over 15 million children in bonded labour, in India today. Twice as many girls than boys engaged in child labour. 63 percent of girls in Delhi, have experienced child sexual abuse at the hands of a family member (Sakshi, 1997).

In a study of 1000 girls from 5 different states in India, 50 percent of the girls said that they had been abused when under 12 years of age, 35 percent had been abused between the ages of 12-16 years of age. The average sex offender has 76 victims. (American data.) There are at least 18 million children living on the streets in India. In a number of joint studies conducted by UNICEF and the Ministry of Labour, In Mumbai 75.4 percent reported bad treatment by staff and 53.2 percent reported that provisions were poor. One million children are trafficked into prostitution.

## 3.13 World Health Organisation Report on Child Abuse

According to the World Health Organisation (WHO), one in every four girls and one in every seven boys in the world are sexually abused. But Lois J. Engelbrecht, a researcher working on the problems of child sexual abuse, quotes studies showing that over 50 per cent of children in India are sexually abused, a rate that is higher than in any other country. Mumbai-based journalist-writer Pinki Virani, for the first time openly came out with facts and figures on sexual child abuse in the year 2000 in her book Bitter Chocolate and broke silence to narrate her own experience of abuse by an extended family member. Her work has also been staged as plays by theatre personality Lushin Dubey. "Two institutions play a very important role in a Child's life when it comes to sexual abuse: there is protection and there is prosecution. Protection is the job of the parent. Prosecution is the job of the state," Virani said in her book.

A girl abused in her childhood by her own family members kept the secret to herself out of fear and shame and it was much later that she recalled the frightful incidents to her boarding school friends. But she was in for a greater surprise: Most of her friends had been victims of some form of sexual abuse during their childhood and had kept it under the wraps, confiding only to their mothers during times of crisis. Sadly, the mothers did all they could to avert the danger but precious little to bring the incidents out in the open.

### Sexual abuse of children in India

Sexual abuse of children is a very real problem in India, and the situation is aided by the absence of effective legislation and the silence that surrounds the offence. The definition of child abuse varies from country to country. Acts that result in physical, sexual or emotional abuse, or neglect of children fall under the purview of law in almost all developed nations. In India, child abuse exists in many forms, but the laws are still ambiguous and most children suffer in silence. In India, which places a high premium on chastity of women and yet has the largest number of child sex workers in the world, there is no single, specific definition of child abuse.

Disbelief, denial and cover-up to preserve family reputation has made child sexual abuse an invisible crime in India. It seems there is an official denial of the existence of the problem. In fact, child abuse in India is as old as the joint family system and patriarchy. Though the problem is highly pervasive, there is pretence that it only inflicts the West. This also explains why there is no framework in India to prevent such abuse and there has not been much data collection and research.

## High Court on child sexual abuse

Alarmed at the growing instances of child sexual abuse, the Delhi High Court has called for a more stringent law for deterrence affect, on 2nd May, 2009 saying the definition of rape under section 376 IPC should be made age and gender neutral. Justice S. Muralidhar was hearing the appeal of a man sentenced to two years imprisonment for committing "digital rape" (inserting finger in vagina) of a five-year-old girl. The judge was upset that lack of

a suitable law prevented the courts from inflicting the same punishment on him as that reserved for a rapist. "The offence of a child sexual abuse is an extremely grave one. Innocent and tender children are abused sexually through a variety of means, one of which is the present case. Such incidents leave a deep scar on the psyche of the child and has the potential of adversely affecting the child's emotional and mental development. The harsh truth is that these incidents are more frequent.

# Chapter-IV
# Female Sufferings

# Female Sufferings

## 4.0 Why get Married?

A couple may be motivated to marry for many reasons other than love and passion. They may want children, enjoy each other's company and trust one another, share interests, outlooks and goals, and find it easy to talk and work together. In the past, women commonly sought financially security, improved status and wealth in marriage. Today many women have careers that fulfil their financial and intellectual needs, women do not necessarily view their role as wife as primary.

People sometimes marry for reasons based on external tension-trying to assert independence from parents, yielding to pressure from their family or peer group, or dealing with an unplanned pregnancy. People may also marry to improve a difficult relationship- unfortunately this rarely has positive results. Motive for marriage - It is widely believed that live and passion are the only valid reasons for two people to marry. In reality, there may be other criteria in operation. Some people decide to marry because they are afraid of being alone.

## 4.1 Marital Discard

The very counter word for marriage is divorce. Divorce is the legal separation of two spouses by bringing an end to the vows that they took during the sacred ceremony of marriage. The divorce procedure differs from one governmental jurisdiction to another. In India divorce is still a major social taboo and divorce seekers have to undergo several ordeals in order to get separated from each other. Unlike Western countries like USA and Sweden, the divorce rate is significantly low in India. In earlier days, in spite of existence of radical disparity between spouses, either of the two was expected to compromise with the other so that their marital bonding survives. In most cases women were forced to adjust with the unbearable post marital conditions for the welfare of the family, the children and even for herself as she was hardly open to any means of earning her own livelihood.

With the advancement of time, spread of education and campaigns of human rights activists, divorce has become a way to break free from the marital clutches for many women. Couples facing difficulties in equating their levels of compatibility are now filing for divorce in order to renew their life afresh. In fact, the rate of divorce is rapidly rising in the Indian Metropolis.

If you are intending to get a divorce from your spouse, the following information will certainly suffice all your inquisitions regarding divorce. Divorce in India is a long legal procedure, whose period of prosecution takes at least six months. The divorce procedure varies from the marriage acts of one personal law to another. All Hindus including Sikhs, Buddhists and Jains can seek divorce under Hindu Marriage Act. Whereas communities like Parsi, Christians, Muslims, have their own laws related to divorce. For example, Christians divorce laws are regulated by the Indian Divorce Act, 1869, and that of a Parsi by Parsi Marriage and Divorce Act, 1936. Inter community marriages are governed by Special Marriage Act, 1956.

## 4.2 Prevention of Marriage Discard

**a) Investigate his background:** Find out the background of the person you and your daughter wants to marry. One way you can do this is by consulting an investing agency. People spend thousands of dollars on marriages but they do not spend a hundred on verification. It would be a great help before hand the kind of denial of marriage bliss. In case of marrying daughter in foreign country, it is very important to verify the credential of the boy whether the boy is married, has a girl friend or has a children. You can find out what social circles he moves. You would know all about a boy who lives either in India or in the US.

Marrying an NRI can be much risker than marrying a boy who lives in India for variety of reasons. It is easy to investigate in home land rather than abroad. There are many men residing abroad wants to seek Indian brides with intention of pleasing their parents. They never think about the feeling and welfare of the girl to marry.

**b) Take time before marriage:** Research has found that many marriages that end up being abusive in relationship. If you take more times to get to know your fiance you have more chances of seeing the warning sign of an abusive man.

**c) Do not marry someone whose family is asking for dowry:** The wedding invitation have already been sent out and your parents are continually harassed for a dowry. In such cases, it is a wise step to discard this proposal in spite of how shameful it might be at the time to withdraw from the marriage.

**d) Do not finalize your plans over long distance through Email or by telephone:** Do not get into any marriage in haste, no matters how much pressure you feel. Marriage is a life transforming event and needs consideration and deliberation.

**e) When marrying in India, register the marriage:** This will ensure that Indian laws can be applied and seek protection in case marriage goes sour.

## 4.3 Sign of Trouble in Marriage

It is best to recognise the sign of trouble, so you can avoid getting into abusive situation and so you get out of an abusive situation as quickly as you are able to identify it as one. Bear in mind that a man who is mentally cruel might be capable of resorting to physical violence. In many instances, a man who shows a desire to control his wife begins with verbal insults and attempts at manipulation and escalates his anger until he lashes out physically. Men control their wives in a variety of ways so it is important to recognize the behaviour that is controlling. Men who are physically and mentally abusive tend to want to know where their wives are at all times and restrict their activities. This restriction of activities is called isolation. If a woman has a little opportunity to do things for herself that are self-enhancing and life-enhancing then that can be taken care.

## 4.4 Divorce Law

India has different divorce laws for different religions. Almost all the religions have their own divorce laws in India which are used among themselves. There are separate laws for inter-cast or inter-religion marriages. Divorce laws in India for Hindus is described in Hindu Marriage Act, 1955. Hindu Marriage Act is also used for Sikhs, Buddhists and Jains as they don't have their own separate marriage and divorce laws. Here is the list of various divorce laws in India for various religions:

* *Hindu (including Sikhs, Jains and Buddists) : Hindu Marriage Act, 1955*
* *Muslims : Dissolution of Muslim Marriages Act, 1939*
* *Christians : Indian Divorce Act, 1869*
* *Parsis : The Parsi Marriage and Divorce Act, 1936*
* *Inter-Cast or Inter-Religion : Special Marriage Act, 1954*

## 4.5 Grounds for Divorce in India

In India divorce is granted mainly on 5 different grounds.

*1. Adultery* *2. Desertion*

*3. Cruelty* *4. Impotency*

*5. Chronic Diseases*

Divorce in India is certainly not an easy procedure. The entire process of divorce that starts from coping up with emotional ups and downs to contesting for the long-awaited divorce decree for several months is definitely a tough affair to get through. Before opting for a divorce, you should be aware of the fact that a divorce procedure in India extents for almost a year and in some special cases of disputes the procedure may continue for years. The long distressing process of divorce will be easier for you to handle if you have a firm determination to get the divorce.

Due to existence of diverse religious faiths in India, the Indian Judiciary has implemented laws separately for couples belonging to different religious beliefs.

With the advancement of time and social awareness, several acts have been passed by the government to make the present-day divorce procedure in India more progressive with respect to gender affairs and related sensitive issues. The Muslim Women Act 1986 was passed to protect the rights of Muslim women on divorce. For inter caste or inter- religion marriages the divorce laws are approved under The Special Marriage Act, 1956.

A contested divorce is filed on the grounds that are mentioned in the acts passed out separately for different Indian religions.

Getting a divorce through mutual consent should always be preferred over the contested divorce as the procedure of getting a mutual divorce is simpler in comparison to that of the other. For a mutual divorce procedure in India, you can come to an agreement with your spouse where you may resolve all kinds of disputes regarding maintenance, custody of children.

Under Section 13B of the Hindu Marriage Act, a husband and wife can file a mutual divorce only when they have lived apart for at least a year. The couple must jointly mention about their inability to continue the marital relationship due to some unavoidable circumstances. Both the sides must voluntarily agree to dissolve the marriage.

The filing of a mutual divorce by both the husband and the wife is termed as 'the first motion'. A couple can file for a second motion after a gap of six months. The six months' time span is provided to the couple so that they get the time to reconsider their marriage.

A divorce decree can be passed before the completion of the six months term if all the mandatory requirements for the divorce are sufficed. If the divorce file is not withdrawn within eighteen months the court passes a divorce decree. In case one of the sides withdraws his/her petition the court initiates to make an enquiry. If the concerned side disagrees to give the consent, the court holds no right to pass the divorce judgment.

Divorce rates in India are the lowest in the world. eleven marriages out of 1,000 marriages (around one marriage out of 100 marriages) ends up to divorce in India. This figure was even low in 1990. In 1990, seven marriages out of 1,000 marriages ended up in divorce in India.

The divorce rate in India is even quite lower in the villages in India and higher in urban parts of India. These days divorce rates in India's urban sphere are shooting up.

In India, marriage is thought to be for life, and the divorce rate is extremely low. Only 1.1% of marriages in India result in a divorce compared with over 45.8% in the United States, though the Indian figure appears to be rising. Opinion is mixed on the implications of this change: "for traditionalists the rising numbers portend the breakdown of society while, for some modernists, they speak of a healthy new empowerment for women."

## 4.6 Parental Right after Divorce

Parental rights are the legal obligations and responsibilities that a parent has for their children. Failing to fulfil the needful duties result in child abuse or neglect, thereby terminating the parental rights legally. But neglecting duties is hardly a matter in India to be considered as enough for terminating parental rights. Termination can be voluntarily or involuntarily, and for various reasons. However, here our concern is to deal with parental rights after divorce.

Child custody is most-sought after aspect of divorce, with each parent trying at their wits end to gain legal guardianship of their child. It is a tormenting whirlpool for parents as well as the child, with parents and extended family trying to influence the child. Though in India, mothers are naturally favoured for legal custody yet court's decision is based on the best interests of child and not the parent's best argument. Guardianship of child is offered to a parent who is seen most fit for the upbringing of the child, providing better financial security, adequate parenting skill and least disruption of the roots of the child.

However, India being a secular country has to respect religious beliefs as well. Hence, personal laws have different notion of physical child custody.

**Custody under Hindu Law:** The secular law for appointment and declaration of guardians and allied matters, irrespective of caste, community or religion, is Guardianship and Welfare Act 1890. Under this act:

- Minor child, under the age of 5yrs., are committed to the custody of mother.
- Older boys to father and older girls to mother, however there is no hard and fast rule and the paramount factor in decision is welfare of the child.

- The choice of child is considered, above the age of 9 yrs. and is only held if it complies with the fulfilment of the welfare requirements of child requirements.
- A mother who is proven to neglect the child in his/her infancy is not handed with the child custody.

**Custody under Muslim Law:** The first and foremost right to have the custody of children belongs to the mother and she cannot be deprived of her right so long as she is not found guilty of misconduct. This right can be held against father or any other person. The father's right of Hizanat is applicable under all Muslim school of laws only in the absence of mother or the completion of age of the child under which the child's custody was committed to the mother.

**Custody under Christian Law:** Christian law does not have any provision for custody but the issues are well solved by the Indian Divorce Act which is applicable to all of the religions of the country.

The concept of welfare of child in India is very broadly designed and followed by the court to ensure custody of child be given to most suited parent. This concept is based on number of factors which are as follows:

- Age, sex and religion of the father of the child plays major role.
- Character and capacity of the proposed guardianship, false accusations and allegation by parents on each other are ignored.
- Any existing or previous relation of the proposed guardian to the minor's property. Minor's inherited wealth play a major role in deciding the custody of child as it can either be weighed against if proven to be the only motto of the custody attainment or in favour if property's owner and proposed guardian are in relation.

- Minor's preference, usually above age of 9yrs., only held if it complies with the fulfilment of the welfare requirements of child requirements. A mother who is proven to neglect the child in his/her infancy is not handed with the child custody.

## 4.7 Sexual Abuse and Marital Rape

Sexual abuse is any situation in which force or threat is used to obtain participation in unwanted sexual activity. Coercing a person to engage in sex, against their will, even if that person is a spouse or intimate partner with whom consensual sex has occurred, is an act of aggression and violence.

Marital rape, also known as spousal rape, is non-consensual sex in which the perpetrator is the victim's spouse. As such, it is a form of partner rape, of domestic violence, and of sexual abuse. In the US spousal rape is illegal in all 50 states; the first state to outlaw it was South Dakota in 1975, and the last North Carolina in 1993.

### Sexual Abuse

- Use of physical force to compel a person to engage in a sexual act against his or her will, whether or not the act is completed.
- Attempted or completed sex act involving a person who is unable to understand the nature or condition of the act, unable to decline participation, or unable to communicate unwillingness.

### Physical Abuse

Physical abuse is abuse involving contact intended to cause feelings of intimidation, pain, injury, or other physical suffering or bodily harm.

Physical abuse includes hitting, slapping, punching, choking, pushing, and other types of contact that result in physical injury to the victim. Physical abuse can also include behaviours such as denying the victim of medical care when needed, depriving the victim of sleep or other functions necessary to live, or forcing the victim to engage in drug/alcohol use against his/her will. It can also include inflicting physical injury on to other targets, such as children or pets, in order to cause psychological harm to the victim, engage in the sexual act, e.g. because of underage immaturity, illness, disability, or the influence of alcohol or other drugs, or because of intimidation or pressure.

## Emotional Abuse

Emotional abuse (also called psychological abuse or mental abuse) can include humiliating the victim privately or publicly, controlling what the victim can and cannot do, withholding information from the victim, deliberately doing something to make the victim feel diminished or embarrassed, isolating the victim from friends and family, implicitly blackmailing the victim by harming others when the victim expresses independence or happiness, or denying the victim access to money or other basic resources and necessities.

Emotional/verbal abuse is defined as any behaviour that threatens, intimidates, undermines the victim's self-worth or self-esteem, or controls the victim's freedom. This can include threatening the victim with injury or harm, telling the victim that they will be killed if they ever leave the relationship and public humiliation. Constant criticism, name-calling, and making statements that damage the victim's self-esteem are also common forms of emotional abuse. Often perpetrators will use children to engage in emotional abuse by teaching them to harshly criticize the victim as well. Emotional abuse includes conflicting actions or statements which are designed to confuse and create insecurity in the victim. These behaviours also lead the victim to question themselves, causing them to believe that they are making up the abuse or that the abuse is their fault.

Emotional abuse includes forceful efforts to isolate the victim, keeping them from contacting friends or family. This is intended to eliminate those who might try to help the victim leave the relationship and to create a lack of resources for them to rely on if they were to leave. Isolation results in damaging the victim's sense of internal strength, leaving them feeling helpless and unable to escape from the situation.

## Verbal Abuse

It is a form of abusive behaviour involving the use of language. It is a form of profanity that can occur with or without the use of expletives.

Abusers may ignore, ridicule, disrespect, and criticize others consistently, manipulate words, purposefully humiliate, falsely accuse, manipulate people to submit to undesirable behaviour, make others feel unwanted and unloved, threaten economically, place the blame and cause of the abuse on others, isolate victims from support systems, harass, demonstrate Jekyll and Hyde behaviours, either in terms of sudden rages or behavioural changes, or where there is a very different "face" shown to the outside world vs. victim.

While oral communication is the most common form of verbal abuse, it includes abusive words in written form.

## Economic Abuse

Economic abuse is when the abuser has control over the victim's money and other economic resources. In its extreme (and usual) form, this involves putting the victim on a strict "allowance", withholding money at will and forcing the victim to beg for the money until the abuser gives them some money. It is common for the victim for those suffering from psychological effects of domestic violence, as it accounts for the variety of symptoms commonly experienced by victims of trauma.

### Financial Implication

Once victims leave their perpetrator, they can be stunned with the reality of the extent to which the abuse has taken away their autonomy. Due to economic abuse and isolation, the victim usually has very little money of their own and few people on whom they can rely when seeking help. This has been shown to be one of the greatest obstacles facing the Victim of DV (Domestic Violence), and the strongest factor that can discourage them from leaving their perpetrators. In addition to lacking financial resources, victims of DV often lack specialized skills, education, and training that are necessary to find gainful employment and also may have several children to support. In 2003, thirty-six major US cities cited DV as one of the primary causes of homelessness in their areas. It has also been reported that one out of every three homeless women are homeless due to having left a DV relationship. If a victim is able to secure rental housing, it is likely that her apartment complex will have "zero tolerance" policies for crime; these policies can cause them to face eviction even if they are the victim (not the perpetrator) of violence. While the number of shelters and community resources available to DV victims has grown tremendously, these agencies often have few employees and hundreds of victims seeking assistance which causes many victims to remain without the assistance they need.

## 4.8 Historical Practises for Females Abuse

Traditions among some communities such as *sati*, *jauhar*, and *devadasi* have been banned and are largely defunct in modern India. However, some cases of these practices are still found in remote parts of India. The *purdah* is still practised by

Indian women among some communities, and child marriage remains prevalent despite it being an illegal practice, especially under current Indian laws.

## Sati

Sati is an old religious practice and largely defunct custom, among some communities in which the widow was immolated alive on her husband's funeral pyre. Although the act was supposed to be a voluntary on the widow's part, it is believed to have been sometimes forced on the widow. It was abolished by the British in 1829. There have been around forty reported cases of sati since independence. In 1987, the Roop Kanwar case of Rajasthan led to The Commission of Sati (Prevention) Act.

## Jauhar

Jauhar refers to the practice of the voluntary immolation of all the wives and daughters of defeated warriors, in order to avoid capture and consequent molestation by the enemy. The practice was followed by the wives of defeated Rajput rulers, who are known to place a high premium on honour.

## Purdah

Purdah is the practice among some communities of requiring women to cover their bodies so as to cover their skin and conceal their form. It imposes restrictions on the mobility of women, it curtails their right to interact freely and it is a symbol of the subordination of women. It does not reflect the religious teachings of either Hinduism or Islam, contrary to common belief, although misconception has occurred due to the ignorance and prejudices of religious leaders of both faiths.

## Devadasis

Devadasi is a religious practice in some parts of southern India, in which women are "married" to a deity or temple.

## 4.9 Dowry Harassment

Pooja Chauhan alleged mental and physical abuse by her husband's family drove 22 years old woman to strip to her underwear and walk through the city in protest. Pooja said she had taken to this unique protest after being constantly harassment for not bringing dowry and bearing a girl child. Pooja had a love marriage but her in laws kept harassing her for dowry, the situation got worst when she had delivered a female child. A police complaint was logged and the family of in laws were arrested.

In 1961, the Government of India passed the Dowry Prohibition Act, making the dowry demands in wedding arrangements illegal. However, many cases of dowry-related domestic violence, suicides and murders have been reported. In the 1980s, numerous such cases were reported.

In 1985, the Dowry Prohibition (maintenance of lists of presents to the bride and bridegroom) rules were framed. According to these rules, a signed list of presents given at the time of the marriage to the bride and the bridegroom should be maintained. The list should contain a brief description of each present, its approximate value,

the name of whoever has given the present and his/her relationship to the person. However, such rules are hardly enforced.

A 1997 report claimed that at least 5,000 women die each year because of dowry deaths, and at least a dozen die each day in 'kitchen fires' thought to be intentional. The term for this is "bride burning" and is criticized within India itself. Amongst the urban educated, such dowry abuse has reduced considerably.

**Rajkot woman stages semi- nude protest against dowry demand**

## 4.10 Dowry Demand Victim at Wedding Night

Partibha, a 22-year-old bride called the police on her wedding night and sent her groom and three others to jail on demanding dowry Rs. 50000/- and threatened that he would take the barat back if her father did not give them the said amount.

While narrating the story of her daughter, the father Ajab Singh with teary eyes said that his daughter was waiting her groom to sit on the stage so that she could be taken there, but the father of groom has refused to let him enter and take the barat back if the dowry amount is not paid to him. Father of bride was begging them with folded hand and even he touched the feet of Sonu's father but he kicked him. When the bride saw the assault on his father, she could not bear with the situation and decided not to marry with him and also decided to call the police and handover them to jail.

Her wedding was fixed with Sonu at ceremony held in Agra, where he ran a stationary shop. Her father said that they gave them a gift and household items worth of Rs. 1 lakh. The family said that they have spent Rs. 2 lakh on the wedding ceremony and want all their gifts back so that they can resettle their daughter who is the eldest of four daughters. Meanwhile, the police produced the accused in court and Rewati Parsad, father of groom kept on saying that they did not ask for the money, they have just asked the bride's family to skip the *varmala* and the *pheras* which has led to a fight.

# 4.11 Suicide by Parent for Dowry Demand for Daughter

## House wife jumps off 8th floor in Dwarika, dies

A 48 year old house wife allegedly committed suicide by

jumping off the eighth floor of multi-storied apartment complex in Dwarika. The victim, Surinder Walia had left behind a "suicide note" which reported that her daughter's in laws were harassing her daughter for dowry just immediately after the marriage, therefore, victim was upset and started reeling under stress. She could not bear the pain of daughter and committed suicide by jumping from 8th floor of her apartment. Surinder Walia's husband said that his wife was very strong and he had no belief that she can take such kind of decision. Basically, under stress or depressed condition, situation stimulates to commit suicide.

# 4.12 Dowry Harassment of Air Hostess

Air Hostess in deadly dowry drama Neetu, 26 years old Air

Hostess alleged that her husband attempted to kill her brother at INA colony in New Delhi. The accused Jitendra Loura, an aerodrome officer with Airport Authority of India absconded and a police case was registered. Neetu had left her in laws, INA colony house due to marital discard. Further, it is alleged that her husband

Mr. Jitendra set her parent's house on fire as evident in photograph. Further, it is stated that her husband also ran over his car on her brother Mr. Bhagat and he was admitted in Ganga Ram Hospital underwent an operation, he sustained injuries all over the body. The accused was arrested and the case was continued in court and he was sentenced to three years jail.

## 4.13 Female Prison Inmates Abuse

Sexual abuse is 'part and parcel' of prison life and harassment of female inmates in exchange for drugs, cigarettes.

**Rhona** (not her real name) is in her late 20s and from Leeds. She says she has "done the circuit" of women's prisons in the North of England and confirms that sexual advances from prison staff - both male and female - are common. In 2005 she was in New Hall prison, near Wakefield, when a male officer "came on strong" to her. It began by him asking her if she had any burn (tobacco). When she said she had none, he gave her three Marlboro Light cigarettes. The next day, he searched for her mobile, some officers are supposed to do it. She says, "For the rest of my stay there - about three months", she thinks - "I would regularly give him hand and blow jobs." Her rewards increased from cigarettes to vodka, which he would bring in plastic bottles. "I was on smack (heroin), which he wouldn't bring in, but I could swap the vodka for gear."

Were other prisoners and staff aware of the relationship? "For sure. He wasn't the only one at it." And did she see the liaison as consensual? "In a way, I suppose. I knew what I was doing; but I wouldn't have looked at him on the outside and only did it for the burn and the vodka. He was a bit arrogant and there were times when I fantasised about biting his cock off."

**Jade Thompson**, 32yrs., is a former drug addict who served several prison sentences for drug-related crimes. Last released in 2003, she has turned her life around, training and working as a drugs abuse support workers. She served time in four prisons - Holloway, Highpoint, Cookham Wood and Foston Hall - and says she witnessed and experienced sexual favours.

**Susan May**, 64yrs., served 12 years of a life sentence for the murder of her aunt in 1992. Released in 2005, she has always maintained her innocence and is currently fighting to get her case referred to the court of appeal for the third time. She has been imprisoned in six different jails.

May agrees with Jade Thompson that Holloway contained a number of predatory female staff. In every jail she was in, she says, there were illicit relationships between staff and inmates. "Some inmates complied, in return for cigarettes and other treats. But many of the younger, more vulnerable women were pressurised, with staff preying on their vulnerability." May says, many women prisoners felt lonely and were more susceptible to the illicit approaches.

**Sara Taylor**, 34yrs., was released from Styal prison in 2007, having served a six-years sentence for robbery. She also spent time at Buckley Hall jail, now a male prison. She says she was frequently propositioned to have sex with both male and female staff during her sentence, and that one male officer promised to let her return to the prison from day release with drugs and alcohol in return for sex. Another asked her to perform a lap dance on him. She said some male officers at Styal would walk quietly to the cell doors and peer through the "Judas hole" - the small hole in a cell door - hoping to catch the women in a state of undress, and that officers would bring CDs and other small gifts for women who supplied them with sexual favours. Ex-women prisoners allege being abused in Jail.

# 4.14 Domestic Violence against Females

## Causes, Consequences and Remedies

"Bride tortured to death for dowry", "School going kid succumbs to his injuries after beaten by father", "A seventy-year-old woman killed over property dispute", "Harassment of woman in Chandigarh".

All these and what not, turn to any newspaper at random and you would find the reports of such kind of violence all over the country. These are all what we come to know through different forms of media. There are more such cases which go unreported every day. In fact, include the cases which we self-indulge in, or the ones which we witness in the neighbourhood but are hesitant in taking even a single step to reduce their occurrences.

In our society, violence is bursting. It is present almost everywhere and nowhere is this eruption more intense than right behind the doors of our homes. Behind closed doors of homes all across our country, people are being tortured, beaten and killed. It is happening in rural areas, towns, cities and in metropolitans as well. It is crossing all social classes, genders, racial lines and age groups. It is becoming a legacy being passed on from one generation to another.

The term used to describe this exploding problem of violence within our homes is Domestic Violence. This violence is towards someone who we are in a relationship with, be it a wife, husband, son, daughter, mother, father, grandparents.

Since times immemorial, Domestic Violence has been an intrinsic part of the society we are living in. The contributing factors could be the desire to gain control over another family member, the desire to exploit someone for personal benefits, the flare to be in a commanding position all the time showcasing one's supremacy so on and so forth. On various occasions, psychological problems and social influence also add to the vehemence. The present essay deals with the various forms of domestic violence prevalent in India. Their causes of occurrence in households have been analysed categorically.

This form of domestic violence is most common of all. One of the reasons for it being so prevalent is the orthodox and idiotic mindset of the society that women are physically and emotionally weaker than the males. Though women today have proved themselves in almost every field of life affirming that they are no less than men, the reports of violence against them are much larger in number than against men. The possible reasons are many and are diversified over the length and breadth of the country. According to United Nation Population Fund Report, around two-third of married Indian women are victims of domestic violence and as many as 70 percent of married women in India between the age of 15yrs. and 49yrs. are victims of beating, rape or forced sex. In India, more than 55 percent of the women suffer from domestic violence, especially in the states of Bihar, U.P., M.P. and other Northern states.

The most common causes for women stalking and battering include dissatisfaction with the dowry and exploiting women for more of it, arguing with the partner, refusing to have sex with him, neglecting children, going out of home without telling the partner, not cooking properly or on time, indulging in extra marital affairs, not looking after in-laws etc. In some cases, infertility in females also leads to their assault by the family members. The greed for dowry, desire for a male child and alcoholism of the spouse are major factors of domestic violence against women in rural areas.

Violence against young widows has also been on a rise in India. Most often they are cursed for their husband's death and are deprived of proper food and clothing. They are not allowed or encouraged for remarriage in most of the homes, especially in rural areas. There have been cases of molestation and rape attempts of women by other family members in nuclear families or someone in the neighbourhood. At times, women are even sexually coerced by their partner themselves against their will. They are brutally beaten and tortured for not conceiving a male child. Incidents like, ripping off a woman's womb for killing the female foetus when she disagrees for abortion have also come to light especially in rural areas. Female foeticide and female infanticide continue to be a rising concern.

Also as expressed by Rebecca J. Burns in the following lines, "When I am asked why a woman doesn't leave abuser I say: A woman stays because the fear of leaving is greater than the fear of staying. They will leave when the fear of staying is greater than the fear of leaving." A common Indian house wife has a tendency to bear the harassment she is subjected to by her husband and the family. One reason could be to prevent the children from undergoing the hardships if she separates.

## 4.15 Domestic Violence against Children/Teens

Children and teenagers in our society are not spared from the evil of domestic violence. In fact, this form of violence is second in terms of number of reported cases after the 'violence against women'. There is a lot of variation in the form of its occurrence in urban and rural areas and in upper/middle class and lower-class families in India. In urban regions, it is more private and concealed within the four walls of homes. The possible reasons could be disobeying parental advises and orders, poor performance in academics or not being at par with other children in neighbourhood, debating with parents and other family members etc. In addition to this, factors like not being socially intelligent or as active as the parents expect them to be, abusing the parents or speaking ill about other family members, not returning home on time are some other factors.

In rural areas the reasons could be harassment for child labour, physical abuse or harm for not following family traditions, forcing them to stay at home and not allowing them to go to school etc. Domestic violence against girls is in fact more severe at homes. As the common mob mentality of India prefers to have at least one male child after marriage, the girls in most of the occasions are cursed and assaulted for having taken birth in the home. This kind abuse is prevalent both in cities and villages but is more common in latter case. Then there are cases of paedophilia causing sexual harassment of children in homes by family member themselves. In fact, the number of rape cases of pre-matured girls has been rising since last few years. A survey of teens and college students found that rape accounted for 67 percent of sexual assaults in girls, apart from sexual abuse and rape,

## 4.16 Domestic Violence against Elderly Woman

This form of domestic violence refers to the violence which old people at home are subjected to by their children and other family members. This category of domestic violence largely goes under-reported in India. It is because of the dependency of olds on their children and having a fear of not being looked after or even ousted if the violence is revealed in public. The main causes of violence against aged people are – children being hesitant in bearing the expenses of the old parents, emotionally victimising the olds and beating them to death.

A perturbing trend is the vulnerability of ageing women to

domestic violence in various forms. Given existing structures of gender discrimination, old women are prone to a greater risk than men of becoming victims of material exploitation, financial deprivation, property grabbing, abandonment, verbal humiliation, emotional and psychological torment. When they fall seriously ill, it is more likely that it is the elderly women in the family who will be denied proper health care. There is also a widespread understanding that the neglect, deprivation and marginalisation of older women are the normal consequences of ageing. In fact, the plight of young widows in homes as discussed above now becomes more serious as a result of the ageing of those women.

## 4.17 Other Forms of Domestic Violence

There are some more possible forms of domestic violence prevalent in India other than the ones listed above. On a serious note, family wars or clan wars are deadly forms of domestic violence across the country. The reasons of such type of violence include dispute over property, physically or emotionally abusing any member of other family or clan, any religious cause or conflict arising during a religious ceremony, jealousy because of progress and financial status of other family, inter-caste marriage etc. This form of violence is common in many States like Haryana, Punjab, Andhra Pradesh etc.

One of the other forms of domestic violence is ill-treatment of servants and maids in households. In many of the affluent homes, servants are deprived of their salary and basic necessities. They are harassed and beaten and to work without even taking adequate rest. Similarly, maids are molested by males in the family. Atrocities against small children working as servants are common and increasing.

To some extent media is also responsible for contributing to all the above forms of violence. The exaggerated news coverage of reports of domestic violence, the daily soaps screening the torture of a daughter-in-law at the hands of family members, the films portraying an element of violence against people of all age groups etc. are some of the menaces which media is causing. It is influencing the mindset of the viewers strongly. The problem arises when instead of taking a lesson from those news clippings, films, and television shows, people start enacting the same in their homes. Comparatively, the visual media is far more influencing than the print and electronic media in these cases. Illiteracy and mob mentality of majority of Indians misguides them in all these cases. people in our midst is growing. A current estimate puts the 60-plus population at around 90 million in India and is projected to have a population of 142 million.

## Effect on the victim and the family

## Consequences of Violence against Women

Battered women have tendency to remain quiet, agonised and emotionally disturbed after the occurrence of the torment. A psychological set back and trauma because of domestic violence affects women's productivity in all forms of life. The suicide case of such victimised women is also a deadly consequence and the number of such cases is increasing.

A working Indian women may drop out from work place because of the ill-treatment at home or office, she may lose her inefficiency in work. Her health may deteriorate if she is not well physically and mentally. Some women leave their home immediately after first few atrocious attacks and try to become self-dependent. Their survival becomes difficult and painful when they have to work hard for earning two meals a day. Many such women come under rescue of women welfare organizations like Women Welfare Association of India (WWAI), Affus Women Welfare Association (AWWA) and Women's Emancipation and Development Trust (WEDT). Some of them who leave their homes are forcefully involved in women trafficking and pornography. This results in acquiring a higher risk of becoming a drug addict and suffering from HIV/AIDS.

One of the severe effects of domestic violence against women is its effect on her children. It is nature's phenomenon that a child generally has a greater attachment towards the mother for she is the one who gives birth. As long as the violence subjected to the mother is hidden from the child, he/she may behave normally at home. The day when mother's grief and suffering is revealed, a child may become upset about the happening deeply. Children may not even comprehend the severity of the problem. They may turn silent, reserved and express solace to the mother. When the violence against women is openly done in front of them since their childhood, it may have a deeper and gruesome impact in their mindset. They get used to such happenings at home, and have a tendency to reciprocate the same in their lives. It's common in especially in rural homes in India which are victimised by the evil of domestic violence.

In cases of Intimate Partner Violence (IPV), violence against women leads them to maintain a distance from their partner. Their sexual life is affected adversely. Many of them file for divorce and seek separation which again affects the life of children.

## 4.18 Sexual Assault and Kidnapping

The 10-year-old Kampusch left her family's residence in Vienna's Donaustadt district on the morning of 2 March 1998, but failed to arrive at school or come home. A 12-year-old witness reported having seen her being dragged into a white minibus by two men. A massive police effort followed, and 776 minivans were examined, including that of Priklopil, who lived about half an hour from Vienna by car in the Lower Austrian town. Although he stated that on the morning of the kidnapping, he was alone at home, the police were satisfied with his explanation that he was using the minibus to transport rubble for the construction of his home.

Speculations of child pornography rings or organ theft were offered, and officials also investigated possible links to the crimes of the French serial killer Michel Fourniret. Kampusch had carried her passport with her when she left (she had been on a family trip to Hungary a few days before) and the police extended the search abroad. Accusations against Kampusch's family complicated the issue even more; there have even been unsubstantiated allegations that Kampusch's mother was somehow involved in the abduction or its cover-up home.

## Captivity of a female child for 8 years

During the eight years of her captivity, Kampusch was held in a small cellar underneath Priklopil's garage. The entrance was concealed behind a cupboard. The cellar only had 5 $m^2$ of space. It had a door made of concrete and was reinforced with steel. The room had no windows, and was soundproof. For the first six months of her captivity, Kampusch was not allowed to leave the chamber at any time and for several years after her kidnapping she was not allowed to leave the tiny space at night. Afterwards, she spent increasing amounts of time upstairs in the rest of the house, but each night was sent back to the chamber to sleep.

However, in later years, she was seen outside in the garden alone, and one of Priklopil's business partners also said that he met Kampusch near his home when her kidnapper, Wolfgang Priklopil, called and came to his home to borrow a trailer. After her eighteenth birthday, she was allowed to leave the house with Priklopil, but her kidnapper threatened to kill her if she made any noise. He later took her on a skiing trip to a resort near Vienna for a few hours. She initially denied that they had made the trip, but eventually admitted that it was true, although she said she had no chance to escape during that time.

According to Kampusch's official statement after her escape, she and Priklopil would get up early each morning to have breakfast together. Priklopil gave her books, so she educates herself, and according to his colleague, she appeared happy. Later, when explaining that in general she did not feel she had missed anything during her imprisonment, she noted, "I spared myself many things, I did not start smoking or drinking and I did not hang out in bad company". But she also said, "I always had the thought, surely I didn't come into the world so I could be locked up and my life completely ruined. I give up in despair about this unfairness. I always felt like a poor chicken in a hen house. You saw my dungeon on television and in the media. Thus, you know how small it was. It was a place to despair." Dietmar Ecker, Kampusch's media advisor, said Kampusch told him, "Priklopil would beat her so badly she could hardly walk. When she was beaten black and blue, he tried to smarten her up. Then he would take his camera and photograph her".

Priklopil had warned Kampusch that the doors and windows of the house were booby-trapped with high explosives.

## Escape from the Captor

The 18 years old Kampusch reappeared on 23rd August 2006.

She was cleaning and vacuuming her kidnapper's BMW 850i in the garden. At 12:53 p.m., someone called Priklopil on his mobile phone, and he walked away to take the call because of the vacuuming noise. Kampusch left the vacuum cleaner running and ran away, unseen by Priklopil, who, according to the caller, completed the phone call without any sign of being disturbed or distracted. Kampusch ran for some 200 metres through gardens and a street, jumping fences, and asking passers-by to call the police, but they paid her no attention. After about five minutes, she knocked on the window of a 71 years old neighbour known as Inge T, saying, "I am Natascha Kampusch". The neighbour called the police who arrived at 1:04 p.m. Later Kampusch was taken to the police station in the town of Deutsch Wagram.

Kampusch was identified by a scar on her body, her passport (which was found in the room where she had been held), and by DNA tests. The young woman was in good physical health, although she looked pale and shaken and weighed only 48 kg. (approximately 106 lbs.), almost the same weight (45 kg.) as eight years earlier when she disappeared. She had grown only 15 centimetres (approximately 6 inches).

## 4.19 Captor- Josef Fritzi, Horror Father

### Captive of a daughter for 24 years in Austria

An Austrian man who held his daughter captive for 24 years and fathered seven children with her had planned the construction of her basement prison years in advance.

Elisabeth Fritzi was kept prisoner for more than two decades. In window less dungeon under the family home, whose original part was built in the late 19$^{th}$ Century, while extension was finished in 1983. Already in the planning phase, there was intension to add something with in this regular building out of sight of the construction authority, a small area, a little secret, a little dungeon. Three of her children had spent their entire lives underground uncovered this information. Elsabeth who says her father started abusing her when she was 11 years old and further stated that her father drugged her and locked up in the basement when she was 18 years old.

The Fritzi case emerged in April, 2008 when a 42 years old woman, Elisabeth Fritzi (born 6$^{th}$ April, 1966), stated to police in the town of Amstetten, Austria, that she had been held captive for 24 years in a concealed corridor part of the basement area of the family home, a condominium-style apartment complex built by her father, Josef Fritzi (born 9th April, 1935), and that Fritzi had physically assaulted, sexually abused, and raped her numerous times during her imprisonment. The incestuous relationship forced upon her by her father resulted in the birth of seven children and one miscarriage.

## Elisabeth Fritzi's confinement

Three of the children were imprisoned along with their mother Elisabeth for the whole of their lives: daughter Kerstin, aged 19yrs., and sons Stefan, 18yrs., and Felix, 5yrs. One child, Michael, died of respiratory problems three days after birth, having been deprived of all medical help; his body was incinerated by Josef Fritzi on his property. The three other children were raised by Fritzi and his wife Rosemarie in the upstairs home. Fritzi engineered the appearance of these children as foundlings discovered outside his house: Lisa at nine months in 1993, Monika at ten months in 1994, and Alexander at 15 months in 1997. When the eldest daughter, Kerstin, became seriously ill, Josef acceded to Elisabeth's pleas to take her to a hospital, triggering a series of events that eventually led to discovery.

## Josef Fritzi's arrest

Josef Fritzi, aged 73yrs., was arrested on 26th April, 2008 on suspicion of serious crimes against family members and went on trial in Sankt Pölten, Austria on 16th March, 2009. He was charged with incest, rape, coercion, false imprisonment, enslavement and the negligent homicide of the infant Michael.

7

8
7

## 4.20 Rape Case in New Delhi

An 18 years old girl was allegedly raped twice at different parts of the city in south Delhi over the span of 24 hours. The incident was reported late that four men have been arrested. According to the complaint filed by the victim, she was first raped by her 42 years old relative in Vasant Kunj, New Delhi and then raped again by a stranger. The victim claimed that when she had managed to escape from her relative's clutches, and had hailed a cab in desperation around 11 p.m., she was again raped by the taxi driver and his two associates.

He added, "Instead of helping her, he took advantage of her vulnerable state, he picked up two other men, Vinod (28yrs.) and Parveen (27yrs.) on the way and they allegedly raped her in the moving car. After that, the two men got down and Bijender drove her to Dwarka sector 19 to drop her off. It was then that a passerby noticed it and made a PCR call around 4.05 a.m. A PCR van sprang into action and managed to apprehend Bijender on the spot."

The other three accused, including Mishra, were also arrested. The girl was taken for medical examination where rape was confirmed, said cops.

Deputy Commissioner of Police (South) claimed that they have managed to arrest all the four accused in less than 24 hours of the incident. Special teams were constituted when this matter was reported, leading to the arrests.

Mishra works with a catering company at the Delhi Airport, while Vinod was a loader there and Parveen was unemployed.

Bijender, Vinod and Parveen were the residents of Barona village in Sonepat, said cops. The victim is reportedly a student of 10$^{th}$ class and a resident of Faridabad. Her brother had recently married Mishra's daughter. A case under IPC sections 376 (rape), 376-2 (g) (gang rape), 366 (kidnapping or abducting a woman) and 368 (wrongfully concealing or keeping in confinement a kidnapped or abducted person) has been registered.

## One of every four rapes in Indian cities take place in Delhi

Delhi has never been very safe for women, and this is not just a perception. The crime figures for the Capital compared to other cities in India, in the year 2009, reveal that almost one-fourth of the rapes were reported from Delhi. Similarly, almost two-fifth of kidnappings/abductions of women happened in Delhi, 15 percent of dowry deaths and 14 percent of molestation cases.

The figures released by the National Crime Records Bureau

(NCRB) of the Home Ministry, show that among 35 Mega cities in India, Delhi reported 404 out of 1,696 rapes; 1,379 out of total 3,544 cases of kidnapping and abduction of women, 104 out of 684 dowry deaths and 491 out of 3,477 cases of molestation during the period under study.

Among the states, the dubious distinction of the "rape state" has gone to Madhya Pradesh which had reported the highest number of rape cases (2,998), accounting for 14 percent of all such cases reported in the country. But if one looks at the figures of 'incest rape' (that is rape by someone in the family), Chhattisgarh reported the highest number of such cases.

## Gang rape case reported from Delhi

New Delhi, 24th June, 2011, just a day after a woman alleged that she was gang raped by five policemen in Inderpuri police station, yet another gang rape case has come to light. A 22 years old woman has alleged that she was gang raped by three men in the Delhi's Shahadra area on Tuesday, 23rd June, 2011.

According to the lady, three men, including her husband's friend, raped her when she was alone at her Bholanath Nagar residence. "I was alone when they entered into the house on the pretext of meeting my husband. They raped and threatened of dire consequences if I made a noise," the woman said in her police complaint. The husband who came home to find his wife crying on the terrace called the police. The police who received the call at around 10 p.m., had reportedly registered a case. The woman had identified the accused and the police nabbed them. The medical reports of the victim had confirmed the rape.

## 4.21 Nirbhaya Case

The 2012 Delhi gang rape and murder case involved a rape

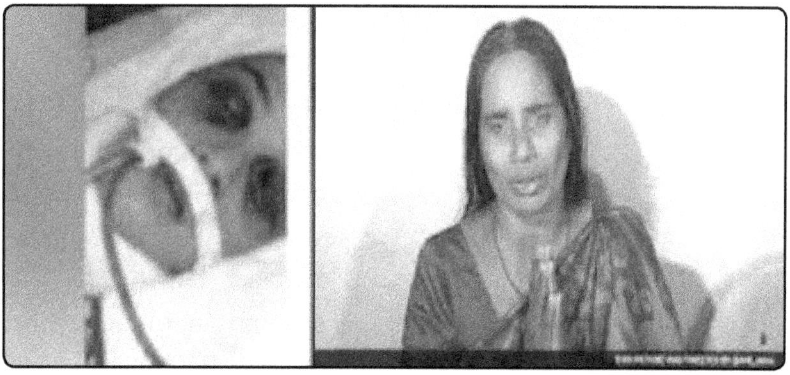

and fatal assault that occurred on 16th December, 2012 in Munirka, a neighbourhood in South Delhi. The incident took place, a 23 years old female physiotherapy intern, was beaten, gang-raped, and tortured in a private bus in which she was travelling with her male friend. There were six others in the bus, including the driver, all of whom raped the woman and beat her friend. Eleven days after the assault she was air lifted to a hospital in Singapore for emergency treatment but died two days later. The incident generated widespread National and International coverage and was widely condemned, both in India and abroad. Subsequently, public protests against the state and central governments for failing to provide adequate security for women took place in New Delhi, where thousands of protesters clashed with security forces. Similar protests took place in major cities throughout the country. Since Indian law does not allow the press to publish a rape victim's name, the victim was widely known as *Nirbhaya*, meaning "fearless", and her struggle and death became a symbol of women's resistance to rape around the world.

All the accused were arrested and charged with sexual assault and murder. One of the accused, Ram Singh, died in police custody from possible suicide on 11th March, 2013. According to some published reports, the police say Ram Singh hanged himself, but defence lawyers and his family alleged he was murdered. The rest of the accused went on trial in a fast-track court; the prosecution finished presenting its evidence on 8th July, 2013. The juvenile was convicted of rape and murder and given the maximum sentence of three years imprisonment in a reform facility, as per the Juvenile Justice Act. On 10th September, 2013, the four remaining adult defendants were found guilty of rape and murder and three days later were sentenced to death by hanging. In the death reference case and hearing appeals on 13rd March, 2014, Delhi High Court upheld the guilty verdict and the death sentences. On 18th December, 2019, the Supreme Court of India rejected the final appeals of the condemned perpetrators of the attack. The four adult convicts were hanged on 20th March, 2020.

# 4.22 Aarushi Case

The Noida double murder case refers to the unsolved murders of 13 years old girl Aarushi Talwar and 45 years old Hemraj Banjade, a male live-in domestic worker employed by her family. The two were killed on the night of 15–16th May, 2008 at Aarushi's home in Noida, India. The case aroused public interest as a whodunit story, and received heavy media coverage. The sensational media coverage, which included salacious allegations against Aarushi and the suspects, was criticized by many as a trial by media.

When Aarushi's body was discovered on 16th May, 2008, the missing servant Hemraj was considered as the main suspect. The next day, his partially decomposed body was discovered on the terrace. The police were heavily criticized for failing to secure the crime scene immediately. After ruling out the family's ex-servants, the police considered Aarushi's parents—Dr. Rajesh Talwar and Nupur Talwar—as the prime suspects. The police suspected that Rajesh had murdered the two after finding them in an "objectionable" position, or because Rajesh's alleged extra-marital affair had led to his blackmail by Hemraj and a confrontation with Aarushi. The accusations enraged the Talwars' family and friends, who accused the police of framing the Talwars in order to cover up the botched-up investigation. The case was then transferred to the CBI, which exonerated the parents and suspected the Talwars' assistant Krishna Thadarai and two domestic servants—Rajkumar and Vijay Mandal. Based on the 'narco' interrogation conducted on the three men, the CBI assumed that they had killed Aarushi after an attempted sexual assault, and Hemraj for being a witness. The CBI was accused of using dubious methods to extract a confession, and all the three men were released after it could not find any solid evidence against them.

In November, 2013, the parents were convicted and sentenced to life imprisonment, but many critics argued that the judgment was based on weak evidence. The Talwars challenged the decision in the Allahabad High Court.

## 4.23 Bhanwari Devi Case in Rajasthan

She was the Dalit hailing from a poor potter's family but in the last decade, Bhanwari Devi has become a torchbearer for the women "movement in the country. Though everyone remembers the name, a few know that even 14 years after she was gangraped by upper caste villagers for attempting to stop a child marriage in her village, Bhateri, about 45 km from Jaipur this lady still has not got justice.

In 1992, as Sathin working for the women's development programme of Rajasthan government, 41 years old Bhanwari tried to persuade a Gujjar family not to marry their one-year old daughter. The police had stepped in and prevented the marriage. However, the marriage took place the next day any way after that the villager ordered socio economic boycott of Bhanwari's family holding her responsible for police intervention.

She was even asked to leave the village but she refused. On 22nd September, 1992, five upper caste men raped Bhanwari in the presence of her husband. The rape was widely seen as punishment for her defiance and because she had challenged accepted cultural norms.

The police had refused to record the complaint and asked to go for medical examination but she had travelled a long distance to go to Jaipur for medical examination. The medical examination reported that there was no evidence of rape. The police investigation held her rape false and said that she was too old to be raped. The case was not filed.

But the pressure of a woman organisation has referred the case to CBI and this case was investigated by CBI and a court case was filed but the Judge acquainted all the five accused because of lack of evidence and also reported that there was delay in complaining the rape and also medical examination was also delayed.

She was unfortunate enough that she could not get the justice till now. This is the fate of the women. It appears that when the justice is not being done to sufferer of such a heinous crime, it is ill fated. This is the law of our country.

## 4.24 Horror Rape Case of Mumbai

Two rape cases have been reported in Mumbai. One of the victims was an aspiring actress and the other was a child of nine years who was reportedly raped after she was dragged from school. A lesser known music video director, R. K. Kumawat has been accused of raping a 25 years old aspiring actress on 22nd July. Police say he lured her with promises of featuring her in a music video.

"Under the pretext of making an item song he had called the girl and then the incident occurred," said Dilip Suryavanshi, Assistant Commissioner of Police, Versova. Kumawat has been remanded to police custody till 29th July. Sources say he admitted the crime during interrogation.

While Kumawat's arrest points towards the menace of casting couch, in another shocking case from another suburb is of a 9 years old girl who was allegedly raped by a 21 years old boy who dragged her from her school to his home where he raped her. "He scared her and took her home where he raped her," said the victim's mother. "He told me not to tell anyone or he'll kill me," said the victim.

The girl was allegedly raped after school on 18th July, but police registered a FIR only on 24th July. The accused has now been arrested and remanded to police custody till 1st August. But without a strong deterrent punishment for rape, this might just be another statistic in a long list.

## 4.25 Crimes Rate in Delhi

Today brought another grim reminder that Delhi, our capital, remains unsafe place for women and girls. New figures released by the National Crime Records Bureau reveal that a shocking one in four rapes in Indian cities take place in Delhi. The city also saw almost two fifths of kidnappings or abductions of women, 15 percent of dowry deaths and 14 percent of molestation cases.

Among 35 Mega cities in India, Delhi reported 404 out of 1,696 rapes. Among large cities, Delhi, Bangalore and Mumbai accounted for 13.2 percent, 9.4 percent and 9.1 percent respectively of the total crimes — over one-third of the total crimes reported from 35 Mega cities.

The new figures, reflecting the latest available data, show that despite efforts an increasing number of women in Delhi are the victims of rapes, assaults and other violent crimes. Unfortunately, these new figures show that the increase in such crimes over the last 15 years is only continuing.

The number of cases of rape reported nationwide has grown at an alarming rate: from 15,031 cases in 1998, to 18,233 in 2004 and a shocking 21,397 in 2009. Delhi has seen the number of cases of rape reported dip since a high of 658 in 2005, but it remains the location of more than double the number of rapes than in other Indian cities, including Mumbai (182), Bhopal (117), and Jabalpur (76).

How can we account for such rises in the number of cases? Whereas some of this may be attributed to better reporting and more women feeling comfortable enough to come forward, other causes may be to blame. These include urban migration, skewed sex ratios due to female foeticide and the shockingly low level of convictions for those accused of rape.

Another possible cause may be the low number of police in the capital city. For a city of over 1.2 crore people Delhi police force consists of only around 57,000 officers. This means that there are only 362 police officers for every 1 lakh people. Overall, India has less than one police officer for every 1,000 people, ranking it 47$^{th}$ in the world overall. Compare Delhi's level of policing with that of London, where a similar number of officers, around 52,000, police a population of only 0.74 crore. Unfortunately, such low levels of policing in the capital cannot alone explain the shocking levels of rape cases reported in the city - other large cities in India have similar numbers of police officers. Mumbai, for example, has only just over 40,000 police officers, with which it must manage a population of over 1.3 crore people. Perhaps a more telling statistic is that of the level of female police officers in Delhi: only 408 officers for a city of over 6 million women.

Some have claimed that it is to other areas that we must look to explain such shocking statistics, and it is to falling standards in public decency that blame for such widespread abuse can be attributed. Perhaps greater liberalisation in what is show on television has had a detrimental effect our collective morality? Since the state monopoly on broadcasting was broken in 1992, India has seen the variety of contents available on cable TV explodes with several recent reality programmes causing widespread controversy with their use of bad language and depictions of intimacy. Through the Cable Television Networks (Regulation) Act of 1995 provides for censorship of unsuitable material, central organised regulation is still lacking, and several experts in the field have expressed a need for setting up of a regulator to regulate content on TV. The number of reported cases of rape has risen steadily from the early nineties when reforms began and cable television started to grow, and have in fact doubled since 1990. But can 'trash TV' really be a contributing factor in such horrendous crimes?

Others have argued that not enough sexual education in schools, or too much, is to blame. Cities in other countries such as Norway, Sweden and Denmark are safer for women, all of which have very different programmes in place. In many such countries sex is not considered taboo in the same way it is in India, and sexual education is compulsory for all children who attend public schools. Obviously, the situation in India is very different. The Supreme Court ruled in 2005 that sex education in schools could not be considered a fundamental right as part of the right to education. The ruling came in response to a petition submitted by the NGO Nari Raksha Samiti, who argued that sex education at schools could play a role in checking the rise in rape cases. Many politicians disagree, with a committee on petitions lead by BJP's Venkaiah Naidu arguing that there should be no sex education in schools, as such classes have not place in the country's "social and cultural ethos".

Many cite a fear that such education would only result in a rise in the level of sexual activity among children and result in more violence towards girls and women. However, the World Health Organisation has said that "Early sex education delays the start of sexual activity, reduces sexual activity among young people, and encourages those already sexually active to have safer sex." Additionally, the WHO has highlighted school programmes on sexual violence as being key to preventing rape and other violence against women.

What else can be done to address this situation? The Government has in the past made efforts to address violence against women in Delhi and to stop the raise in the cases of rape reported. In 2004, the Delhi Commission for Women stated, "To make Delhi more secure for women, to provide a safer climate for women and to strive towards building confidence amongst women is the Government's foremost concern." Whereas the introduction of services such as the Commission's rape crisis cell and the support given to NGOs providing similar services is to be applauded, one cannot escape the conclusion that much, much more needs to be done.

The raising number of rape cases reported in the capital only reflects wider societal attitudes towards the place of women. In addition to working on improving conviction rates and making it easier for women to report cases, the wider attitudes and beliefs of the Indian public must be tackled. If we all collectively address the various areas in which the women of all of India face discrimination, from female foeticide and public harassment to work place discrimination and child marriage, we can begin to realise true equality and make all our cities safer for everyone.

## 4.26 Aruna Shanbaug Case of Mumbai

Aruna Shanbaug hailing from Haldipur town of Uttar Kannada district in Karnataka, was a junior nurse, at King Edward Memorial Hospital in Mumbai and was planning to get married to a medic in the hospital.

On the night of 27th November, 1973, Shanbaug was sexually assaulted by Sohanlal Bhartha Balmiki, a ward boy at the King Edward Memorial Hospital. Balmiki was motivated partly by resentment for being ordered about and castigated by Shanbaug. Balmiki attacked her while she was changing clothes in the hospital basement. He choked her with a dog chain and sodomized her. The asphyxiation cut off oxygen supply to her brain, resulting in brain stem contusion injury and cervical cord injury apart from leaving her cortically blind.

The police case was registered as a case of robbery and attempted murder on account of the concealment of anal rape by the doctors under the instructions of the Dean of KEM, Dr. Deshpande, perhaps to avoid the social rejection of the victim and her impending marriage.

Balmiki was caught and convicted, and served two concurrent seven-year sentences for assault and robbery, neither for rape or sexual molestation, nor for the "unnatural sexual offence" (which could have got him a ten-year sentence by itself).

## Supreme Court Case

Since the assault in 1973, she had been in a vegetative state. On 17th December, 2010, Supreme Court while admitting the plea to end the life made by activist-journalist Pinki Virani, sought a report on Shanbaug's medical condition from the hospital in Mumbai and the Government of Maharashtra. On 24th January, 2011, the Supreme Court of India responded to the plea for euthanasia filed by Aruna's friend journalist Pinki Virani, by setting up a medical panel to examine her.

The three-member medical committee subsequently set up under the Supreme Court's directive, checked upon Aruna and concluded that she met "most of the criteria of being in a permanent vegetative state." However, it turned down the mercy killing petition on 7th March, 2011. The court, in its landmark judgement, however allowed passive euthanasia in India. While rejecting Pinki Virani's plea for Aruna Shanbaug's euthanasia, the court laid out guidelines for passive euthanasia. According to these guidelines, passive euthanasia involves the withdrawing of treatment or food that would allow the patient to live.

## Response

Following the Supreme Court judgment rejecting the plea, her colleagues, the nursing staff at the hospital, who had opposed the petition, and who have been looked after her, since she lapsed into coma, distributed sweets and cut a cake to celebrate what they termed here birth". Senior nurse at the hospital later said, "We have to tend to her just like a small child at home. She only keeps aging like any of us, does not create any problems for us. We take turns looking after her and we love to care for her. How can anybody think of taking her life?"

Pinki Virani's lawyer, Shubhangi Tulli ruled out filing an appeal stating "the two-judge ruling was final till the SC decided to constitute a larger bench to re-examine the issue". Pinki Virani herself stated, "Because of this woman (Aruna Shanbaug), who has never received justice, no other person in a similar position will have to suffer for more than three and a half-decade."

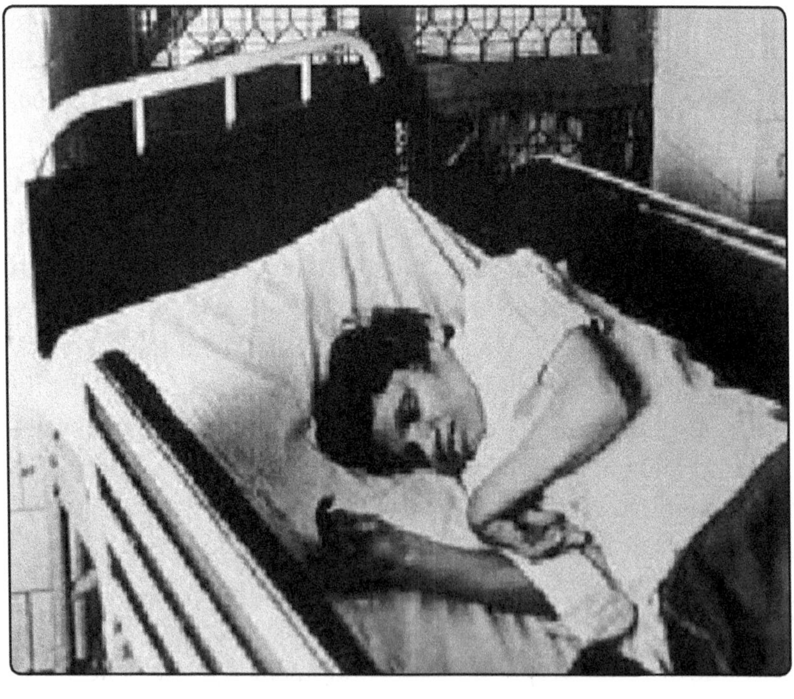

## 4.27 Female Trafficking

The scale and extent to which women and children are trafficked to, from and within India and her neighbouring countries remains relatively little-explored, despite the grave effects of a practice which condemn many to lives of servitude or slavery. Women and girl children remain particularly vulnerable to trafficking within and into India, partly due to the adverse sex ratio that creates a deficit of women in certain regions of the country. Regions with fewer women, such as Punjab and Haryana, become the eventual destinations for women and girls trafficked from poorer states such as Assam, Jharkhand and West Bengal. Trafficking seals the fate of many of India's poorest women: Whether enticed by the prospect of employment or sold by their own families, trafficking victims are sentenced to a life of bonded labour, forced marriage or occasionally forced prostitution. In turn, they are further deprived of their most basic human rights, including the rights to physical and mental health and the right to be free from torture or degrading.

Thailand and the Philippines have 1.3 million children in its sex-trade centres. The children come from relatively poorer areas and are trafficked to relatively richer ones. In cross border trafficking, receiving children from Bangladesh and Nepal and sending women and children to Middle Eastern Nations is a daily occurrence. India and Pakistan are the main destinations for children under 16yrs. who are trafficked in south Asia. More than 40 percent of 484 prostituted girls rescued during major raids of brothels in Mumbai in 1996 were from Nepal. In India, Karnataka, Andhra Pradesh, Maharashtra, and Tamil Nadu are considered major states for women in prostitution. Bajpur, Belgaum and Kolhapur are common districts from which women migrate to the big cities, as part of an organised trafficking network. Districts bordering of Maharashtra and Karnataka, known as the *devadasi belt*, have trafficking structures operating at various levels. The women here are in prostitution either because their husbands deserted them, or they are trafficked through coercion and deception. Many are devadasi dedicated into prostitution for the goddess Yellamma. In one Karnataka brothel, all 15 girls are devadasi.

Women and children from India are sent to Nations of the Middle East daily. Girls in prostitution and domestic service in India, Pakistan and the Middle East are tortured, held in virtual imprisonment, sexually abused, and raped. In Mumbai, children as young as 9 are bought for up to Rs. 60,000 or US$2,000 at auctions where Arabs bid against Indian men who believe sleeping with a virgin cures gonorrhoea and syphilis. 1,60,000 Nepalese women are held in India's brothels. Approximately 50,000 or half of the women in prostitution in Mumbai, are trafficked from Nepal. The brothels of India hold between 1,00000 and 1,60,000 Nepalese women and girls, 35 percent were taken on the false pretext of marriage or a good job. About 5,000-7,000 Nepalese girls are trafficked to India every day. 1,00000-1,60,000 Nepalese girls are prostituted in brothels in India. About 45,000 Nepalese girls are in the brothels of Mumbai and 40,000 in Calcutta.

Calcutta is one of the important transit points for the traffickers for Mumbai and to Pakistan. 99 percent women are trafficked out of Bangladesh through land routes along the border areas of Bangladesh and India, such as Jessore, Satkhira, and Rajshahi. In shelters in India, there are 200 Bangladeshi women and children who have been trafficked awaiting repatriation. Of the 5,000-7,000 Nepalese girls trafficked into India yearly, the average age over the past decade has fallen from 14-16 years old to 10-14 years old. In Mumbai, one brothel has only Nepalese women, men buy because of their golden skin and docile personalities. 2.5 percent of prostitutes in India are Nepalese, and 2.7 percent are Bangladeshi. Some Indian men believe that it is good luck to have sex with scalp-eczema afflicted prostitutes. Infants with the condition, called "pus babies," are sold by their parents to brothels for a premium. 70% of students surveyed at a wealthy high school seek a career in organized crime, citing their reasoning as "good money and good fun."

## Trafficking in Thailand

Around 80,000 women and children have been sold into Thailand's sex industry since 1990, with most coming from Burma, China's Yunnan province and Laos. Trafficked children were also found on construction sites and in sweatshops. In 1996, almost 2,00000 foreign children, mostly boys from Burma, Laos and Cambodia, were thought to be working in Thailand. (Mahidol University's Institute of Population and Social Research, "Trafficking of children on the rise," Bangkok Post, 22nd July, 1998) Pattaya has a multi-billion-dollar multinational sex industry with links to drug trafficking, money laundering and an expanding regional cross-border traffic in women.

## Methods and Techniques of Traffickers

Victims of trafficking from other nations are easily deceived or lured because they face poverty, unemployment, broken families and unstable governments in their own countries. Girls in China are kidnapped and trafficked through Burma to Thailand. In one kidnapping scheme in the central Thai provinces, an agent photographed village girls on their way to school; showed the photos to a brothel keeper who ordered the girls he wanted. The agent returned and kidnaped the chosen girl. The networks in Thailand involved in the trafficking of women have liaisons in Japan, Singapore, Taiwan and Hong Kong. Thailand is a staging point for the International Trade in

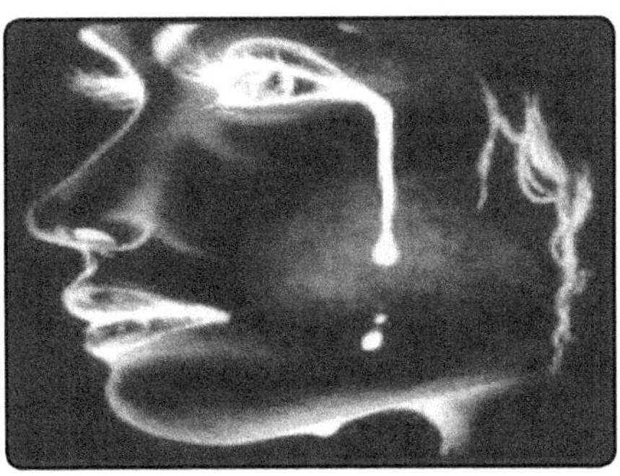

prostitutes and illegal workers, with facilities for the production of false travel documents and processing of Foreign Nationals to third countries.

Russian women, looking for a better life and to escape from the Russian economic crisis, are being trafficked to Pattaya in Thailand. Most of the women became involved with job placement agencies offering high-paying work as dancers, waitresses, domestic servants or sale representatives. Trafficking networks in Russia charge the women anywhere from $1,500 to $3,000 (60,000 to 1,20,000 Baht) and once in Thailand, the women are kept in constant fear. Their passports are taken away on their arrival. The women are forced to work long hours for little pay and threatened with death or the death of their families if they don't cooperate.

Most European women in prostitution in Thailand are from Russia, the Czech Republic and Romania. The women enter via procurers in Thailand and their native Nations.

## 4.28 Asaram Bapu Case

Self-styled godman Asaram Bapu was booked for allegedly raping one of two Surat-based sisters who stayed at his ashram in Gujarat between 1997 and 2006. In a charge-sheet filed against him in a Gandhinagar court, the spiritual guru has also been accused of illegal confinement and criminal conspiracy. Five others, including his wife and daughter, have also been booked by the police.

This is the second case of sexual assault against Asaram Bapu, who is lodged in a jail in Rajasthan since August last year.

He was arrested on charges of sexually assaulting a teenage girl at his Asaram in Jodhpur. Later, two Surat-based sisters who stayed at his ashram in Gujarat accused him and his son Narayan Sai with regard to rape case. In her complaint, the elder of the two sisters has accused ashram of repeated sexual assault during the time she lived in his ashram on the outskirts of Ahmedabad city. Asaram Bapu has denied all charges against him. (Asaram Bapu raped teen, aides helped organise the crime, says police). His son Narayan Sai, against whom the younger of the two sisters has registered a complaint of sexual assault, is currently lodged in a jail in Surat.

The son of self-styled and controversial godman Asaram Bapu, Narain Sai, has confessed to raping a woman, to having relations with various women and fathering a child, said a senior officer of Surat police on Wednesday.

Surat police commissioner Rakesh Asthana said, "He has accepted more or less the main allegation of rape. He has admitted that he fathered a son of Moksha (name changed). He has not divulged information, and for that, he will seek further remand. Apart from it, he has also admitted eight relationships, which will be investigated. Earlier, a court had remanded Sai to police custody in sexual assault case for five days till 11th December. The crime branch of the Delhi police had arrested Sai on 4th December.

Two sisters from Surat had filed a police complaint alleging that Sai and his father had raped them. Asaram aged 72yrs. was arrested on 1st September on allegations of sexual assaulting a teenage girl at his Ashram in Jodhpur, Rajasthan. A Jodhpur court is all set to pronounce the verdict in a high-profile rape case involving self-styled godman Asaram Bapu. She had accused him of raping her at his Jodhpur ashram. The victim was a student at Asaram's ashram. He was later booked under stringent sections of the POCSO Act and SC/ST Act.

## 4.29 Tehelka Case-Tarun Tejpal

Tehelka founder and editor Tarun Tejpal, accused of sexually assaulting a woman journalist, on Thursday filed an application before a local court demanding an in-camera hearing of his bail petition. Reportedly, Tejpal's lawyer moved the application for in-camera hearing before the district and sessions court when the case was on board for arguments on his bail plea. The arguments on his petition asking for an in-camera hearing were heard today and the court will announce its verdict tomorrow. The court will subsequently hear his bail petition.

Tejpal, 50 years old accused of sexually assaulting a former junior woman colleague in a hotel here in early November, was arrested by Goa police on 30$^{th}$ November, 2013. He had been booked under IPC sections including 354-A (sexual harassment, physical contact, advances involving unwelcome and explicit sexual overtures,) the court observed, dismissing one Tara Dutt's appeal. Charged with sexually assaulting his junior colleague inside an elevator of a resort hotel in Goa during an event organised by the magazine in November, 2013, Tejpal has been booked under Sections 376 (rape), 341 (wrongful restraint), 342 (wrongful confinement) 354A (sexual harassment) and 354B (criminal assault), of the Indian Penal Code.

## 4.30 Patriarchy and Prevention of Violence

Being a male affords an individual many privileges in the Indian patriarchal society. The opposite holds true for the female sex and gender. A patriarchal society is one which is organized and built upon relationships and structures where men wield power and dominance. Patriarchy – more simply defined as "rule of the fathers" – is a "form of social organization in which cultural and institutional beliefs and patterns accept, support, and reproduce the domination of women and younger men by older or more powerful men." This male-centric society inherently puts girls and women at risk of exclusion and marginalization simply on the basis of their sex and gender.

Patriarchy manifests itself in the societal norms of "son preference" in India where a disproportionate number of girl children continue to fall prey to female foeticide and infanticide. Most Indian households continue to prioritize the nutrition, health, education, housing, and opportunities for livelihoods for male children over female. Boys and men are raised with a sense of entitlement including how they are socially conditioned to treat girls and women as inferior, unequal and to be controlled.

Given this conditioning, it is not surprising that gender-based violence against girls and women is routinely normalized and accepted. India's National Family Health Survey (NHFS-4) showed that every third woman in India between the ages of 15-49 has faced physical, sexual, or emotional violence with the violence being perpetrated by a close family member or a spouse in the case of married women. While a greater number of cases were reported from rural areas, women in urban India are not immune from facing sexual and physical abuse. The many rape and sexual assault cases that have been reported from major metropolitan Indian cities in the recent years are a case in point.

Violence prevention in such a context requires the Indian society to reimagine its social and cultural norms and practices and breaking down of the patriarchal structure that normalizes the treatment of girls and women as dispensable members of society. It is important to understand that patriarchy hurts boys and men too. It puts inordinate pressure on the male members of society to "act like a man" or "be a man" often at the cost of their emotional wellbeing because they are neither expected to nor encouraged to show their vulnerability or emotional fragility. It burdens men to disguise the truth that boys and men too are vulnerable to and experience sexual and physical abuse. Patriarchy limits boys and men in their ability to fully be their authentic selves and openly express their hopes and aspirations for a life beyond that of being a provider for their households and families. Patriarchy puts boys and men at risk of engaging in toxic masculinity where brute aggression, power and control are priced over love, care, and empathy.

For patriarchal structures to be broken down and replaced, it is important to start with the unlearning of existing social and cultural norms. We need to see a social commitment to nurturing boys and girls with the same standards starting from the moment a child is conceived. We need a social contract that welcomes each birth irrespective of the sex and gender of the child born. We need to raise our boys and girls with equal access to all the basic needs as well as opportunities that will help them grow into healthy, well-adjusted and contributing members of society. We need to ensure that each household sees an equal distribution of labor in terms of domestic duties and responsibilities and no undue burden is placed on a woman to be the home maker and the man to be a bread winner. Most importantly, we need to nurture gender equality and equity where men and women collectively shape the future of the human race with care, love and grace.

As American Author, feminist and social activist Bell Hooks famously wrote, "Love cannot exist in any relationship that is based on domination and coercion. Males cannot love themselves in patriarchal culture if their very self-definition relies on submission to patriarchal rules. When men embrace feminist thinking and practice, which emphasizes the value of mutual growth and self-actualization in all relationships, their emotional well-being will be enhanced."

Violence prevention starts at home, with each of us making a commitment to being part of the change.

# Chapter-V
# Prostitution in India and Abroad

# Prostitution in India and Abroad

## 5.0 Prostitution in India and Abroad

There are approximately 10 millions prostitute in India. There are more than 1,00000 women in prostitution in Mumbai, Asia's largest sex industry entreat least 2,000 women are in prostitution along the Baina Beachfront in Goa. There are 3,00000-5,00000 children in prostitution in India.

Men who believe that AIDS and other STDs can be cured by having sex with a virgin, are forcing young girls into the sex industry; 7 years old girls are neither uncommon nor the youngest. Approximately 20,000 or 20 percent of women in prostitution Mumbai are under 18 years old. Every day, about 200 girls and women in India enter prostitution, 80 percent of them against their will.

Karnataka, Andhra Pradesh, Maharashtra, Tamil Nadu and Uttar Pradesh high percentage of women are in prostitution. Belgaum, Bijapur, and Kolhapur are some common districts from which women migrate to cities either through an organized trafficking network, or due to socio-economic forces.

Bangalore is one of the five major cities in India which together account for 80 percent of child prostitutes in the country. 90 percent of the 1,00000 women in prostitution in Mumbai are indentured slaves. Prostitution is increasing in India where there have been fears over the spread of AIDS and reports of young girls being abducted and forced into prostitution. It takes up to fifteen years for girls held in prostitution via debt-bondage to purchase their freedom.

Children of prostitutes are victims of sexual abuse as well. Children are forced to perform dances and songs for male buyers, and some are forced to sexually service the males. Of 1,000 red light districts all over India, cage prostitutes are mostly minors, often from Nepal and Bangladesh. In Mumbai, 95 percent of the children of prostitutes become prostitutes. One child, who had repeatedly been sodomized by the men who bought his mother, decided to become a eunuch. He was ritually castrated. There are three routes into prostitution in India. Deception, Devadasi dedication and failed marriages or families. For some women their marriages were so violent they preferred prostitution. Husbands or families introduced some women to prostitution. Many families knew what the women had to do, but ignored it as long as they got the benefits from it. The red-light district in Mumbai generates at least $400 million a year in revenue, with 1,00000 prostitutes servicing men 365 days a year, averaging 6 customers a day, is the Falkland Road Kamathipura area of Mumbai.

In Kamathipura brothel more than 70,000 prostituted women and girls are bought by three men a day. Condoms are seldom used. Escape is rare. There are many dhabhas, or small-scale brothels, along the Solapur-Hyderabad highway, which provide women as an "additional service" to truck drivers and motorists. One woman who runs a dhabha had previously been in prostitution. Now, with a shed, two cots and a few girls from nearby villages, she owns the brothel and rented this place for Rs. 1000 a month and take Rs. 20 per man from the girls.

A brothel owner along the Solapur-Hyderabad highway reported that he has two women. He takes a Rs. 15 as a commission from each man. Since this is illegal, he pays the nearest police station Rs. 1,000 a month as hafta, or bribe. If a girl is beautiful, she will be bought by five to ten men a day. The owner's monthly earnings can reach Rs. 4,000 to 5,000 per month.

A brothel owner along the Solapur-Hyderabad highway reported that prostituting women is good a business. He had ten to 12 girls. He paid the police Rs. 6,000 as a monthly bribe. He goes to Mumbai to bring women and girls, implying he was the part of a bigger network.

The women and girls in the dhabhas or brothels, along the Solapur-Hyderabad highway, are threatened, harassed, forced to service men, or goondas, freely and beaten by men and police. Local farmers abuse them also. Police do not register any complaints of assault. In one of cases, a woman who was running over unfamiliar fields to escape the police in pitch darkness, she stumbled into a well and was killed. Sometimes, bodies of women are found on the fields, half eaten by animals. Another woman had her ears cut off, was robbed and left unconscious on the road.

Eunuch Lane in Mumbai has more than 2,000 eunuchs in prostitution. The eunuchs or *hijras*, have deep religious roots in Hinduism. As young boys they are abandoned or sold by their families to a sex ring and taken into the jungle, where a priest cuts off their genitals in a ceremony called nirvana. The priest then folds back a strip of flesh to create an artificial vagina. Eunuchs are generally more available to perform high-risk sex than female prostitutes, and some Indian men believe they can't contact HIV from them.

A survey of prostitutes in India reveals their reasoning for staying in prostitution poverty/ unemployment, lack of proper reintegration services, lack of options, stigma and adverse social attitudes, family expectations and pressure, resignation and acclimation to the lifestyle.

## Health and Well-being

Madams take sick women to one of the red-light districts 200 unlicensed doctors, who give the women mood elevators, drips of coloured water or medicinal herbs. The women must pay for this "treatment" with cash from moneylenders, and the Mafia collects a percentage from the "doctors." 60 percent of prostituted women in Mumbai's red-light district areas are

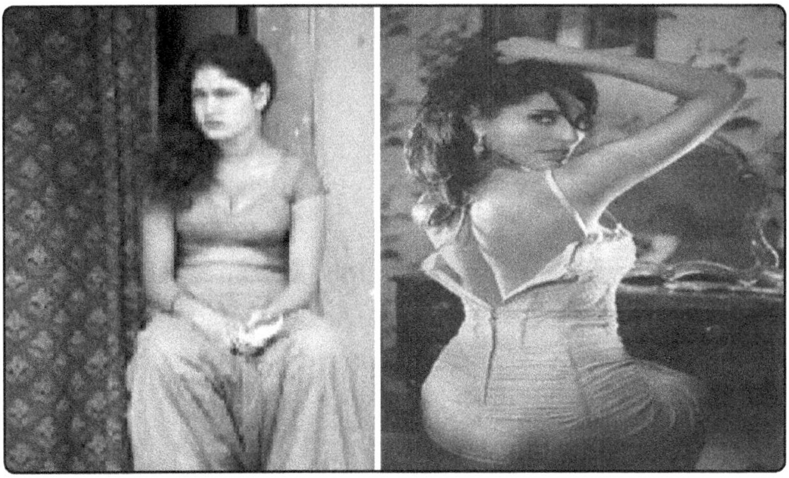

infected with STDs and AIDS. More than half of Mumbai's 1,00000 prostitutes are infected with HIV. A magazine publisher in Mumbai said AIDS will benefit the country because it will depopulate the vast underclass.

In July 1990, mob bosses permitted Savadhaan India, a charity group, to repatriate 700 South Indian prostitutes to Madras, most of whom were HIV positive. It was perceived as a cheap way of getting rid of HIV infected girls. Many women, too sick to prostitute are thrown on to the street. Government hospitals won't treat prostitutes who are HIV positive, or are developing symptoms of AIDS. In Mumbai's J.J. Hospital an HIV infected woman was refused treatment, though she was bleeding and her condition was life threatening. She delivered a baby in the brothel.

In Mumbai, on an average the girls are brought by six men a day, who pay US $1.10 - $2 per sex act, the madam gets commission. To pay for movies, clothes, make-up and extra food to supplement a diet of rice and daal, the girls have to borrow from moneylenders at an interest rate of up to 500 percent.

## Prostitutes Luring on roads of Hyderabad

Sex with high grade prostitutes was a costly affair and has run

with a secret brothel houses, this is the past story. Hyderabad has now become the so called "Metro" by inheriting the foreign "Metro" culture. With raising incomes and ever-increasing demands to satisfy your libido, the sex services are now available at your door step now, says an analyst. By the time when clock returns to 11 p.m., major centres like RTC Cross road, Punjagutta Circle, Secunderabad Railway Station, Nagarjuna Circle, Gymkhana ground and other major areas are flourishing with tempting prostitutes and service-oriented pimps.

Police even with good knowledge of these happenings just stay away from this situation. Whole of the city comes alive with traffic and regular activities by 4 a.m., but these illegal sex activities will begin their day from 11 p.m. or 12 a.m. mid night. It is the ill fated customers of Hyderabad that even eunuchs started to make hot money by staying on the roads alluring two wheelers and four wheelers with their jatakas. Be careful, when you get out of your house after 11 p.m. by any mistake.

## Prostitution of Children

Prostitution of children or child prostitution is the commercial sexual exploitation of children in which a child performs the services of prostitution, for financial benefit. The term normally refers to prostitution by a minor, or person under the local age of majority. In many countries there are specific laws against child prostitution which may include people who are older than the local age of consent. The form of child prostitution in which people travel to foreign countries for the purposes of avoiding laws in their country of residence is known as child sex tourism.

A customer may negotiate an exchange directly with a child prostitute in order to receive sexual gratification, or through an intermediary (pimp) who controls or oversees the prostitute's activities for profit. The provision of children for sexual purposes may also be an object of exchange between adults. Many children are prostituted over the Internet with the use of webcams to facilitate this abuse, and child pornography may be linked to the site of Pros Asia.

In Cambodia, it has been estimated that about a third of all prostitutes are under 18 years. The exact number of child-prostitutes in Thailand is not known, but Thailand's Health System Research Institute reports that children in prostitution make up 40 percent of prostitutes in Thailand. In India, the federal police say that around 1.2 million children are believed to be involved in prostitution. A CBI statement said that studies and surveys sponsored by the Ministry of Women and Child Development estimated that about 40 percent of all India's prostitutes are children.

An article in the Gulf Times revealed a major sex trade in mostly Nepalese boys who were lured to India and sold to brothels in Mumbai, Hyderabad, New Delhi, Lucknow and Gorakhpur. One victim was lured from Nepal at the age of 14 years, sold into slavery, locked up, beaten, starved and forcibly circumcised. He reported that he was held in a brothel with 40 to 50 other boys, many of whom were castrated. He escaped and made his way back to Nepal. Two Non-Government Organisations, one that work with homosexuals in Nepal, and one that works to rescue and rehabilitate trafficked women and children were co-operating to help these boys. In Indonesia, UNICEF estimates that 30 percent of the female prostitutes are below 18 years.

In Sri Lanka, there are nearly 40,000 child prostitutes, according to UNICEF and ILO. In Philippines, there are 60,000 to 1,00000 children in prostitution, according to UNICEF and non-governmental organisations. In Nepal, according to research conducted by the International Labour Organization (ILO) on 440 prostitutes from Kathmandu, approximately 30 percent of them were found to be children. In Bangladesh, the UN Children's Fund (UNICEF) estimated in 2004 that there were 10,000 under age girls used in commercial sexual exploitation in the country, but other estimates placed the figure as high as 29,000. There are estimated to be at least 70,000 prostitutes in Vietnam, and 20,000 of these are children. In Afghanistan,

Bacha Bazi is a form of child prostitution employed by Afghan warlords where small boys are regularly bought and sold into sexual slavery.

## South America

By 1999, it was reported that in Argentina child prostitution was increasing at an alarming rate and that the average age was decreasing. The CATW fact book says Argentina is one of the favoured destinations of paedophile (A person who is sexually attracted to children) sex tourists from Europe and the United States. The criminal code criminalizes the prostitution of minors of eighteen years of age or younger, but it only sanctions those who "promote or facilitate" prostitution, and not the client who exploits the minor. It is estimated that Peru has about 5,00000 child prostitutes. In Colombia, it is estimated that there are 35,000 child prostitutes, with between 5,000 and 10,000 of them on the streets of Bogota. In Chile the estimated number of children involved in some form of prostitution has decreased. In 1999, UNICEF informed that there were approximately 10,000 children between the ages of 6yrs. and 18yrs. involved in prostitution, but in 2003, a Government Agency estimated that there were approximately 3,700 minors. In Ecuador, a 2002 International Labour Organization report estimated that 5,200 minors were engaged in prostitution. In Bolivia, the average age of entry into prostitution is 16yrs. Brazil is considered to have the worst child sex trafficking record after Thailand. According to the Protection Project Report, various official sources agree that from 2,50,000 to 5,00000 children live as child prostitutes, but other sources in Brazil put the number up to 20,00000 children.

## 5.1 Prostitution in New Delhi

**Prostitution racket busted five Uzbek girls**

A high- profile prostitution racket was busted by the South

District Police in New Delhi after the arrest of of five Uzbekistan call girls. The police claimed that one International gang is involved in supply of girls and also came to know that the racket provided in-house facility on extra payment. The police claimed to have information about the racket and police raided and arrested the pimps and five girls under different sections of immoral trafficking act and foreigner act. The interrogation revealed that the girls used to visit India for short duration for the purpose of prostitution. they hire independent floor in posh colony of Delhi and build their clientele.

# Chapter-VI
# Female Murder, Accident and Suicide

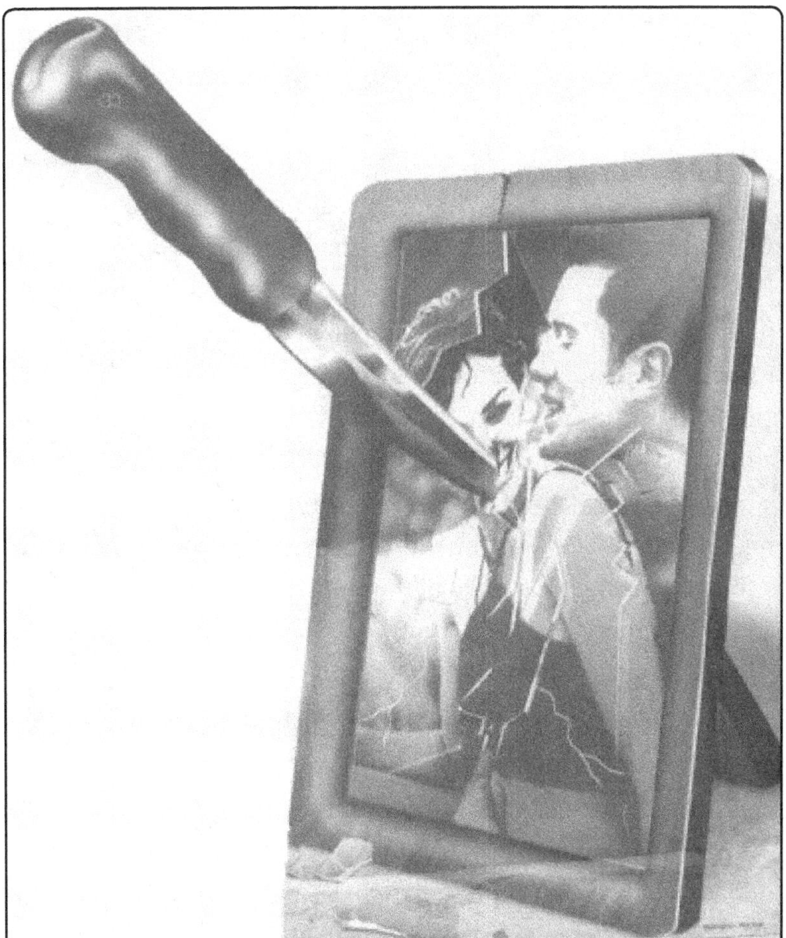

# Female Murder, Accident and Suicide

## 6.0 Radhika Tanwar Murder Case

The main suspect in the Radhika Tanwar murder case had

been arrested from Mumbai. 20 years old Radhika was shot outside her college in South Delhi on Tuesday. On Friday, the Delhi police had identified the alleged killer as Vijay alias Ram Singh, a "mentally unstable" man who might have been involved in such an incident before. According to police, Vijay has confessed his crime, saying he knew Radhika's route to college, and was waiting near the bridge on 8$^{th}$ March, to kill her. Police claim he had followed Radhika several times before, but his immediate provocation came three days before the crime, when he tried to speak to Radhika at the same foot over bridge, where he later shot her.

According to the cops, Vijay bought a gun from Gurgaon, and chose to shoot her on the foot over bridge where the ramp ended, so as to make a speedy exit from the crime scene. He even ran 500 metres with the gun in his hand, without anyone trying to catch him. Vijay used to work at a knitting unit near Radhika's house, and reportedly teased and followed girls in the area - he was beaten up twice for this behaviour.

He shifted to Mumbai three years back, but would keep coming to Delhi and try and follow Radhika each time. Radhika's family is relieved that the police have caught the killer, but say they still do not believe in the stalker theory. "We first want to see him and get him verified by her friends and then we will be convinced," said Rajinder Singh, Radhika's father. At later stage after finalisation of case in court, the killer was sentenced to jail for 10 yrs.

## 6.1 Naina Sahni Tandoor Murder Case

In the night of 2nd July, 1995, Delhi police constable Abdul Nazir Kunju and home guard Chanderpal saw smoke emanating from the open-air Bagiya Restaurant in Ashok Yatri Nivas (now called Indraprastha hotel). They got suspicious and scaled the hotel's boundary wall to enter the premises. 'Something big' was burning in a tandoor (a clay oven) in the restaurant. That 'something big' turned out to be the body of Naina Sahni (29 years old), who was allegedly killed by her husband and the then Delhi Youth Congress President Sushil Sharma. Since the flames were touching the restaurant's ceiling, the two, in order to stop it from spreading, doused the fire with water. Later, while deposing in court, Kunju and Chanderpal stated that the restaurant manager Keshav Kumar claimed- 'he was burning Congress banners'.

In 2001, investigation officer Niranjan Singh told a website: "We have a fool proof case against the accused. The motive of the crime was clear from the very beginning - the accused doubted Sahni's character. Their marriage was under tremendous pressure as he was torturing her. He didn't want their marriage to be made public. Sahni wanted to leave Sharma and go abroad."

Sahni's parents wanted it (the trial) to end. Asked for an interview in 2001, her 77 years old father, Harbhajan Singh, said that why do you want to talk about her? She has gone and nothing can bring her back. You can't solve anything. Can you get me justice? Tell me, what kind of a father am I, who couldn't get justice for his daughter? Let me forget it all. Don't remind me of her running the restaurant on a contract and was present when the body was being disposed off, managed to flee. He surrendered on 10th July, 1995. The two had been languishing in judicial custody ever since three other co-accused were out on bail.

According to the 19-pages charge sheet submitted by the police, Sharma doubted Sahni's fidelity. He believed she was having an affair with her classmate and fellow Congress worker Matloob Karim. This suspicion led to marital discard and the police alleged domestic violence. Besides, Sharma wanted to keep his marriage with Sahni a secret, which the latter opposed. On 2nd July, when Sharma reached his flat at Mandir Marg in the heart of the capital, he saw Sahni talking on the telephone. Seeing him, she put down the receiver. Sharma re-dialled the number to find out who was on the other end. His suspicion was confirmed when Karim answered the phone. Incensed, Sharma allegedly fired three shots from his licensed revolver at Sahni. One bullet pierced her head, another hit her in the neck while the third missed her and hit an air-conditioner. Police team led by Additional Commissioner of Police Maxwell Pereira flew to Chennai, but Sharma fled to Bangalore, where he surrendered on 10th July, 1995. When the case went to trial, Sharma and Kumar pleaded innocence.

The murder had sent shockwaves across the capital. Tandoors being ubiquitous in Delhi, it was hard to go to a restaurant and not discuss the case, which has seen as many twists as can be expected in the Indian Judicial System, New Delhi. The Delhi High Court has ordered the release of Sushil Sharma, a former politician, who is serving life sentence since 1995 for murdering his wife Naina Sahni. The high-profile murder case had become famous as the "*Tandoor Kand*".

## 6.2 Shivani Murder Case

**Shivani Bhatnagar** (died on 23rd January, 1999) was a journalist working for the *Indian Express* newspaper. Her murder on 23rd January 1999 became a scandal that reached into the top levels of Indian politics. Indian Police Service officer Ravi Kant Sharma was charged with the murder by the Delhi police, who investigated the case. Sharma surrendered to the police on 27th September, 2002, after having been in hiding since the arrest warrant was issued on 3rd August of that year. Sharma allegedly got Bhatnagar killed because he feared she would expose their "intimate" relations.

IPS officer Ravi Kant Sharma along with Sri Bhagwan Sharma, Satya Prakash and Pradeep Sharma were accused in the Shivani Bhatnagar murder case and they were convicted by a Delhi Trial Court on 18th March, 2008. Two other accused—Dev Prakash Sharma and Ved Prakash alias Kalu—were acquitted for want of evidence. Those convicted were sentenced to life imprisonment on 24th March, 2008. On 12th October, 2011, Delhi High Court acquitted Ravi Kant Sharma, Sri Bhagwan Sharma and Satya Prakash saying lack of evidence on appeal. The conviction of Pradeep Sharma was upheld.

## 6.3 Jessica Lal Murder Case

Jessica Lal (1965–1999) was a model in New Delhi, who was working as a celebrity barmaid at a crowded socialite party when she was shot dead on 29th April, 1999. Dozens of witnesses pointed to Siddharth Vashisht, and Manu Sharma, the son of Venod Sharma, a wealthy Congress Politician in Haryana, as the murderer. In the ensuing trial, Manu Sharma and a number of others were acquitted on 21st February, 2006.

Following intense media and public pressure, the prosecution appealed and the Delhi High Court conducted proceedings on a fast track with daily hearings during the summer of 1999, leading socialite Bina Ramani had been organizing "Thursday Special" nights, at her newly opened "Tamarind Court" restaurant, at Qutub Colonnade, a refurbished haveli overlooking the Qutub Minar in Mehrauli.

On 29th April, 1999, it was the seventh and last Thursday special of the season; also being celebrated was the foreign visit of Bina Ramani's Canadian husband Georges Mailhot, for a period of six months. Though the restaurant was yet to receive its liquor license, drinks could be bought through discreetly marked 'QC' coupons, and on that night, several models and friends were serving drinks at the 'Once Upon A Time' bar, including Jessica Lal, Bina Ramani's daughter Malini Ramani, friends Shayan Munshi, and others.

Previously, at 10 p.m., Manu Sharma alias Siddharth Vashisht, the 24 years old son of former Union Minister Venod Sharma, having skipped his planned visit to Chandigarh, drove up to the Friends Colony house of Amrinder Singh Gill (Tony), 32 years, a General Manager of the Coca-Cola bottling unit in Delhi, where they were joined by 30 years old Alok Khanna, a colleague of Tony, and Vikas Yadav, son of Rajya Sabha Member, it was a busy night, the drinks were soon over, at about 2 a.m. Manu Sharma asked for a drink, which Jessica refused, he then tried to offer a thousand rupees, which she refused as well. Though there are many versions of what happened next, sometime soon, the inebriated and enraged Manu Sharma shot at Jessica twice at point blank range, the first bullet hitting the ceiling. The second one proved fatal, as it hit Jessica, who was now kneeling over, on the temple and she fell unconscious immediately. Twenty minutes later, she was rushed to the Ashlock Hospital (in Safdarjung Enclave) in a car but she succumbed to her injuries that same night at the Apollo Hospital. The police brought the body to AIIMS for post-mortem examination. Dr. R.K Sharma and Dr. Sudhir Gupta were the AIIMS Autopsy Surgeons & gave important forensic opinion to the prosecution in this case at various stages.

Vikas Yadav slipped away from the scene together in Alok's car, while Manu Sharma hid for a while in a nearby village, a kilometre away. The trio dropped Amit Jhingan at his Vasant Kunj residence, and reached Tony's Friends Colony residence, where later Manu Sharma also joined them, after hitchhiking his way there on a two-wheeler. There he was given the weapon for hiding. Manu Sharma spent the night at Vikas Yadav's Ghaziabad residence, later, their escape vehicle, a Tata Sierra, was found abandoned in Noida.

While Manu Sharma and most of his family continued to abscond, as did Venod Sharma and his family, Alok Khanna and Amardeep Singh Gill (Tony) were arrested on 4th May. On 8th May, Bina Ramani, her husband, George Mailhot and her daughter Malini, were arrested under the Excise Act for running an illegal bar after interrogation; also arrested was Manu Sharma's accomplice, Amit Jhingan, from Vasant Kunj under Section 201 read with 120 (conspiring to destroy evidence), on the basis of disclosures made by Manu Sharma during interrogation. A Delhi court granted bail to the Ramanis, though their passports were seized, with Bina being a British National, her husband, a Canadian National, and Malini a US National; and Amit Jhingan was remanded to judicial custody till 21st May. On 19th May, Vikas Yadav walked into the Delhi police headquarters and surrendered, but only hours later he walked out, as he carried anticipatory bail papers from Imphal Court. The police chose not to arrest him.

On 3rd August, 1999, Delhi police filed the charge sheet in the court of Metropolitan Magistrate, wherein Manu Sharma was named the main accused and charged under sections 302 (murder), 201 (destruction of evidence), 120(b) (criminal conspiracy), and 212 (harbouring suspects) of the Indian Penal Code; and sections 27, 54 and 59 of the Arms Act. While other accused, like Vikas Yadav, Coca-Cola Company officials Alok Khanna and Amardeep Singh Gill (destroying evidence of the case and conspiracy); Shyam Sunder Sharma, Amit Jhingan, Yograj Singh, Harvinder Chopra, Vikas Gill, Raja Chopra, Ravinder Krishan Sudan and Dhanraj, were all charged variously under sections 120(b), 302, 201 and 212 of the IPC (for giving shelter to the accused and destroying evidence).

Manu Sharma gave a statement to the Police, which was taped, in which he admits shooting Jessica Lal. "The idea at that time was to shoot in challenge. It was embarrassing to hear that even if I paid a thousand bucks, I would not get a sip of drink." This audiotape was obtained and aired by the TV channel NDTV, but it does not constitute legal testimony. Subsequently, however, the confession was retracted, and a not guilty plea was entered in the trial.

Delhi LG allows release of Jessica Lal murder convict Manu Sharma. Son of former Union minister Venod Sharma, was convicted and sentenced to life imprisonment by the Delhi High Court in December 2006 for killing Jessica Lal in 1999.

# 6.4 British Teenager Murder Case

Schoolgirl Scarlett Keeling was found dead with bruises on her body at Anjuna Beach in Goa on 18th February, 2008. An autopsy report revealed that Harvey had died from a pulmonary and cerebral oedema, but detectives were investigating whether drugs or violence could have played a part in her death. Her body was found in the morning after she checked in to Ben's Inn on Aswem beach. She was the tenth Briton to die in Goa this year. A post-mortem investigation found sand in Scarlett's mouth but little water in her lungs. "The fact is that my daughter did not drown in the sea but died of asphyxia when her face was pushed into the sand by her assailants," said Mrs. Mac Keown. "The body of my daughter was found on the sand and not in the sea, as falsely stated by the police. Scarlett poses with an elephant in Goa in the days before her murder, her body was found naked, yet the police informed me

she was in her swimwear. "There are a large number of abrasions on her body, yet the police tried their best to convince me as well as the media that the body did not have any abrasions. They have lied all the way through." Scarlett, from Bideford, Devon, had been on a six-month backpacking holiday with her mother, her mother's partner Rob and her six brothers and sisters, arrived in Goa on 22$^{nd}$ November, 2007.

After fighting for the truth behind her daughter's death, Mrs. Mac Keown believes it is even possible police were involved in Scarlett's rape and murder. She said, "Three weeks back an Australian female tourist was relaxing in the south Anjuna Beach after dark. She did not possess any contraband but was bodily searched and then raped by men in uniform. "When she went to the police station in Anjuna the duty officer dissuaded her from lodging a complaint, explaining that such a complaint would cause huge harassment to her before she could get justice. She left the country without officially reporting the matter. "A large number of tourists from countries including England, Italy, Germany, Australia and France have shared their experiences with me, verbally and on email."Scarlett was last seen alive with two "unsavoury characters" at Lui's Cafe on south Anjuna beach at 4 a.m. of 18$^{th}$ February, 2008. Her body was warm when discovered nearby at 6.30 a.m.

## 6.5 Nithari Case of Serial Murders

The Noida serial murders (also Nithari serial murders) took place in the house of a businessman Moninder Singh Pandher in Nithari, Noida in 2005 and 2006. At present his servant Surender Koli had been convicted of four murders and sentenced to death. Twelve murders remain officially unsolved pending further legal proceedings.

On December, 2006, two Nithari residents claimed they knew the location of remains belonging to children who had gone missing in the previous two years. Two daughters of a Nithari villager who had disappeared, and they suspected Surender Koli, the domestic help at D5, Noida, had something to do with the disappearances. The residents claimed they had been repeatedly ignored by local authorities; therefore, they sought the help of former Resident Welfare Association (RWA) President S. C. Mishra. That morning, Mishra and the two residents searched the tank drain, and one of the residents claimed to have found a decomposed hand, after which they called the police. Anxious parents of the missing children rushed to Nithari with photographs. Koli, under the alias Satish, later confessed to killing six children and a 20 years old girl known as "Payal" after sexually assaulting them.

The residents alleged that the police were corrupt and involved with the rich people. Demands were made for an independent probe into the matter. One of the residents asserted that the police were claiming credit for discovering the bodies when it was the residents who dug them up. The police denied having found fifteen bodies. They reiterated that they had discovered skulls, bones and other body parts and said they were unable to give a figure for the number of victims. The victim's identities and number could only be established with DNA tests. The police then sealed the house and did not allow news media anywhere near the scene of crime.

The Central Government tried to ascertain the facts behind the discovery of the skeletal remains and whether it had "inter-state ramifications". Law and order is a state's subject but the Home Ministry asked for details about the magnitude of the crime.

It was later revealed by the media that Koli's employer, Moninder Singh Pandher, was picked up by the police on 26th December and Koli on 27th December in connection with the disappearance of "Payal". After Koli's confession, the police claimed to have started digging up the nearby land area and discovered the children's bodies.

Two policemen were suspended on 31st December in connection with the serial murders as angry residents charged the house of the alleged mastermind. The policemen were suspended for dereliction of duty in the wake of the allegations by the locals that the police had refused to take any action when they were informed about a number of children missing.

The situation at Nithari got aggravated as an irritated mob of villagers fought pitched battles with the police, both pelting stones to each other, just outside the residence of the accused. The police also detained a maid named Maya whom they suspected had a hand in procuring women for the businessman. As more body parts were dug out from near the premises of the house, hundreds of local residents descended on the spot and alleged that there was an organ trade angle to the grisly killings of young children. A doctor living close to the Pandher's residence, Navin Choudhary, had been under police suspicion a few years prior in connection with an alleged kidney racket at his hospital. Raids were conducted throughout the properties owned by him, and the investigators could not derive any information to support the claim.

## Primary investigation

On 1st January, 2007, the remand magistrate granted the

police custody of the two until 10th January, 2007, as the investigators said that further interrogation was required to complete the recovery of victims' remains. The court also granted permission for Narco Analysis. On the same evening, police conducted a raid on Pandher's Chandigarh residence. His wife and son were interrogated and questions were asked about Pandher's habits. Police sources disclosed that their relationship with him was "strained", which was later found untrue. His behaviour was "normal". A senior police inspector revealed that there would be a series of searches conducted at Pandher's Ludhiana farmhouse and nearby places. The recent child kidnapping cases in Chandigarh—Pandher's hometown—were re-opened and nothing was found.

It was on the next day that 15 out of 17 skeletons discovered in the village were identified. Ten of them were identified by Koli when he was confronted with the photographs of the missing children. Five others were identified by family members after being shown belongings recovered from the scene. The torsos of the bodies were missing and the investigating team was looking into possibilities of the motivation of the killings to be that of organ trade. The police said that there were at least 31 victimised children.

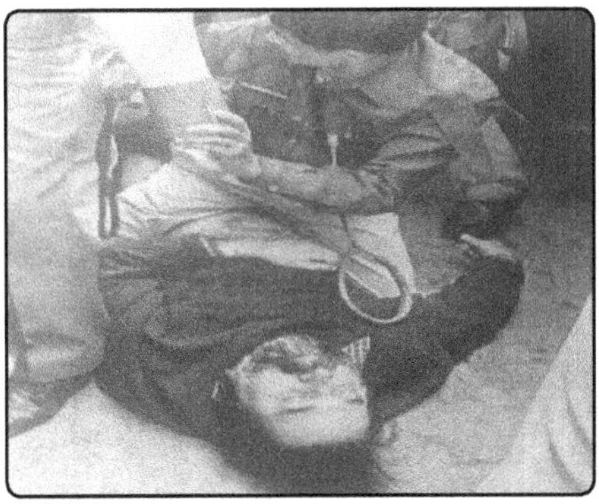

Security was increased as police expected more disturbance, following two days of violence near Pandher's residence. In a press statement, Chief Justice of India Y. K. Sabharwal asserted that the investigation was at a preliminary level, and neither the courts nor the Central Bureau of Investigation (CBI) were involved at that point. Both the accused were given the death sentence on 13$^{th}$ February, 2009 as the case was classified "rarest of rare". I personally visited at the site during the raid of police at house D-5, Noida, Uttar Pradesh.

# 6.6 Acid Attack on Females

Laxmi Agarwal (born on 1st June, 1990) is an Indian acid attack survivor, a campaigner for rights of acid attack victims, and a TV host. Agarwal was attacked in 2005 at the age of 16yrs., after rebuffing the romantic advances of Naeem Khan. Her story, among others, was told in a series on acid attack victims by *Hindustan Times*. She has since established grassroots campaigns for tackling the surge of acid attacks; one of her petitions has led the Supreme Court to order the central and state governments to regulate the sale of acid and the Parliament to enable easier prosecutions of acid attack perpetrators. She was the former Director of Chhanv Foundation, a NGO dedicated to help acid attack survivors in India.

In 2019, she was honoured with the International Women Empowerment Award from the Ministry of Women and Child Development, the Ministry of Drinking Water and Sanitation, and UNICEF for her campaign of *Stop Sale Acid*. In 2014, she received the International Women of Courage award at the hands of First Lady Michelle Obama.

## Public interest litigation in Supreme Court

Agarwal, whose face and other body parts were disfigured in the acid attack, had public interest litigation (PIL) in 2006. A minor then, she was attacked with acid by three men near Tughlaq road in New Delhi as she had refused to marry Naeem Khan, Aka Guddu, one of the trio. Her PIL sought framing of a new law, or amendment to the existing criminal laws like IPC, Indian Evidence Act and CRPC, for dealing with the offence, besides asking for compensation. She also pleaded for a total ban on sale of acid, citing an increasing number of incidents of such attacks on women across the country.

During a hearing in April, the Centre assured the Supreme Court of India that it would work with the state governments to formulate a plan before the next hearing on 9th July. However, it failed to do so, which angered the court. However, when the Centre failed to produce a plan, the Supreme Court warned that it would intervene and pass orders if the government failed to frame a policy to curb the sale of acid in order to prevent chemical attacks. "Seriousness is not seen on the part of the Government in handling the issue," the bench headed by Justice RM Lodha said. Earlier, in February, the court had directed the Centre to convene in six weeks a meeting of Chief Secretaries of all states and Union Territories to hold discussion for enacting a law to regulate the sale of acids and policy for treatment, compensation and care and rehabilitation of such victims.

Meanwhile, in 2013, the Supreme Court ruled in favour of Agarwal and Rupa's plea, thereby creating a fresh set of restrictions on the sale of acid. Under the new regulations, acid could not be sold to any individual below the age of 18 years. One is also required to furnish a photo identity card before buying acid.

Agarwal claims that not much has changed on the ground, despite all the regulations. "Acid is freely available in shops. Our own volunteers have gone and purchased acid easily. In fact, I have myself purchased acid," she said. "We have launched a new initiative called 'Shoot Acid'. By means of the Right to Information Act, we are trying to acquire data concerning the sale of acid in every district. We intend to present the information collected through this initiative before the Supreme Court to apprise them of the situation on the ground."

## Personal life

Agarwal was in a relationship with social activist Alok Dixit. However, she has been separated from her partner since 2015, When they were together, Dixit decided not to get married and instead opted to be in a live-in relationship. "We have decided to live together until we die. But we are challenging society by not getting married. We don't want people to come to our wedding and comment on Laxmi's looks. The looks of a bride are most important for people. So, we decided not to have any ceremony," said Dixit. Their families have accepted the relationship and also their decision not to have a ceremonial wedlock.

## 6.7 Niagara Falls Death in Canada

Ayano Toumasus, a 20 years old Japanese student, who was studying English in Toronto University, Canada swept over Niagara fall. On 14th August, 2018. Police said that surveillance footage from a nearby visitors centre showed a young woman holding an umbrella, straddling a safety railing and gazing at the falls, it appeared that as if she was having her picture taken by a friend, but when she got up to climb back over the railing, she lost her balance and slipped into the rushing waters near brink of Horseshoe falls. Five Police and fire department on both sides of border tried to search for the whole night but body was not discovered. Young woman presumed dead.

**Ref. Toronto Star News Paper, Canada, 15th August, 2018**

## 6.8 Electrocuted in Car Accident in Canada

A young girl was driving her car at very high speed to

celebrate New Year on 1st January, 2017, in Toronto. While trying to turn on iced road, she dashed to a electric pole carrying transmission line of 15,000 volts at a very high speed. The electric pole fell on her car. There was no option to escape from car charged with high voltage but to jump from the car but could not escaped, she was badly electrocuted and she got unconscious placed in coma.

In Canada, roads are being monitored by satellite, visual cameras and helicopter, Canada Police immediately located the area of accident and they rushed to the spot with Ambulance and carried the girl to nearby hospital for medication. After the medication, she recovered her consciousness and become in position to talk to doctors. They, after reviewing the condition of patient found that all her four limbs were to be amputated because of electric shock. Doctors asked the option /consent whether she has a will to die or amputation of four limbs. She had consented for amputation of all four limbs because she wanted to live her life even being handicapped. This is the motivation in life. She survived and presently living in Toronto, Canada.

**Ref. Toronto Star News Paper, Canada dtd. 2nd January, 2017**

## 6.9 Suicide by Models

The supermodels lead outwardly glamorous lives, the pressure to stay in shape and on top proves fatal for someone. The life of model can be not only fiercely competitive, often living alone. Many young models come from other countries or different states of India have difficulty getting acclimated to a new culture. Lack of confidence, peace and tranquility might be the reason to end their lives. Further to add that models can feel that they are loved for their beauty and figure, if they become more beautiful, they will be more loved. But instead of that, they feel used and then there are feeling of betrayal. There might be other reasons related to mental health because of overdoing, no rest, stress, strain, anxiety and pressure to supersede to their seniors. In this competitive world, these things are expected to happen. The purpose of life is to save your life by all means whatever may be the situation or any unwarranted circumstances. In life, it is important that the possession should not possess us, we should possess the possession.

**Rakhee** **Saumya** **Natasha** **Ritu** **Divya**

❑❑❑

# References

1. Google Search Engine
2. Outlook Magazine
3. Times of India
4. Hindustan Times
5. Navbharat Times (Hindi)
6. Toronto Star News Paper dtd. 2nd January, 2017 and 15th August, 2018
7. Zee News Channel
8. India TV Channel

*This photo is taken from Art Gallery of State Hermitage Museum, St. Petersburg, Russia. The Author personally visited there in 1993*

Edited this book on 'Meaning of life' authored by my grand child 10 yrs. old Citizen of Canada

'Book on blog' authored by Ashok Kumar Rai in 2020

Edited book on 'Envoirnment Management in Thermal Power Generation' authored by Shri TK Dhar, Ex. Executive Director, NTPC

Authored this book on 'Stress Management', released by Sri Sri Ravi Shankar, Guru of Art of Living, on 5th Nov. 2005 and complimented by Ex President late Abdull Kalam and Prime Minister Shri Narender Modi.

Edited this book 'Essence of ( Mis) Management' authored by Late GS Sohal, ED NTPC

Edited book on 'Rehabilation & Resettlement Polices' authored by Shri Mahanand Jha, Ex, Executive Director, NTPC

www.ingramcontent.com/pod-product-compliance
Lightning Source LLC
LaVergne TN
LVHW011812181026
850499LV00040BA/1366
* 9 7 8 9 3 9 0 2 8 7 9 3 2 *